THE COMPLETE
START-TO-FINISH
LAW SCHOOL
ADMISSIONS GUIDE

By Jeremy Shinewald of **jdMission**

D0360528

Manhattan Prep Publishing • New York

The Complete Start-to-Finish Law School Admissions Guide

Published by Manhattan Prep Publishing, Inc.
138 W 25th St, 7th Floor
New York, NY 10001
www.manhattanprep.com/publishing

Copyright © 2012 by Manhattan Prep Publishing, Inc., New York, NY

ISBN-10: 1-935707-99-X
ISBN-13: 978-1-935707-99-8
eISBN: 978-1-937707-35-4

Layout Design by Dan McNaney and Cathy Huang
Cover Design by Dan McNaney
Cover Photography by Ashly Covington

To Samantha, Moishe, and Boulder

ABOUT JDMISSION

jdMission's elite admissions consulting services give law school applicants a competitive edge as they strive to secure a place in the school of their dreams. All our consultants are graduates of top law schools as well as profoundly experienced writers and editors, and are devoted to helping applicants identify and communicate the distinct characteristics that will distinguish them from the rest of the applicant pool. With one-on-one guidance and assistance, we work tirelessly to help our clients maximize their chances of admission and achieve their law school goals. Your legal career begins with jdMission.

TABLE OF CONTENTS

INTRODUCTION

§ INTRODUCTION

Almost a decade ago, literally only a few days after I had officially launched my career as an admissions consultant, I received a call from an international phone number. The voice on the other end of the line asked whether I worked with clients on law school applications, particularly those clients seeking an LLM (Master of Laws degree). The individual told me that he wanted to apply to Harvard Law School but that he was without a clue as to how to write his personal statement and his statement of research interests—could I help?

Over the next few weeks, I assisted this candidate with crafting the details of his personal journey from the military to law school and then helped him write the statement of research interests required for his LLM, explaining his particular intellectual connection to the legal issues inherent in exercising a completely arcane European financial instrument (we will leave it at that—the explanation is not crucial to this introduction). After he got into Harvard's LLM program, he came back to me wanting to apply for a scholarship, and in the end, he earned $20,000 from a quasi-governmental organization in his home country. One year later, he and I worked together on his PhD applications, and he was again accepted to Harvard.

He was one of my first JD clients, and while I helped him gain acceptance to his target school, he in turn helped me understand an important truth. It was not my job to understand arcane financial information, but to guide others in telling their stories in a way that compels the admissions committee to take notice. I knew the best ways to reveal his passion for life and his area of academic interest, and that was what was most important.

Years later, I have assisted numerous candidates with getting into top law schools—Harvard, Yale, Northwestern, Chicago, New York University, and the list goes on. Although we can do little to help candidates with the important quantitative elements of their candidacies (namely, LSAT scores and GPAs), we can absolutely guide them in effectively communicating their strengths, sharing their unique stories and minimizing their weaknesses, all while doing our best to ensure they stand out positively from the pack.

The thrust of this book is therefore on the "art" of applying to law school. It begins with a chapter on the basics of the application process to lay a foundation for our guidance, and in the next five chapters, it delves into the intricacies of this "art." We find that law school applicants often fail to view their candidacies in an overarching, holistic way, and our goal here is to make sure you truly make the most of *all* aspects of the application process. So, we encourage you to do your best on the LSAT and hope that you performed well as an undergraduate, but our focus in this book is on the impression you can make on the admissions committee via your personal statement, diversity statement, addenda, recommendations, résumé, and other facets of your application that you may not have considered yet. This book also offers some insight into what being a law student and embarking on a legal career really entail, so you can look forward with more information in hand.

This book was written to give you the tools necessary to craft a compelling law school application and prepare for this next exciting phase of your career. If you feel that you need more "hands-on" help, however, we at jdMission are always available to work with you one-on-one to put these concepts into practice and help improve your chances of attending the law school of your dreams.

Sincerely,

Jeremy Shinewald
Founder/President, jdMission

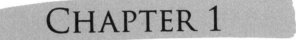

CHAPTER 1

What You Need to Know about Applying to Law School

In the coming chapters, we will delve into the details of how to shape your essays, résumé, recommendations, and other important elements of your law school application. But, beforehand, we want to take a step back and offer a basic overview of the entire process of applying to law school. Because this process can often be incredibly competitive—top-ranked Yale Law School accepts less than 10% of applicants each year, for example—candidates tend to fixate on just the quantifiable, and thus more easily comparable, aspects of their applications, namely their LSAT score(s) and GPA. As a result, they do not consider as thoroughly the other aspects of their profile (work experience, personal accomplishments, recommenders, etc.) or the other elements of the process, such as the right time to submit one's application and the way schools typically evaluate candidates. Although the LSAT and GPA data points are undeniably crucial, thinking about your candidacy on a more holistic basis will result in a stronger—and ideally, more successful—application. In this chapter, we will take the proverbial bull by the horns and attempt to dispel some law school application myths, while giving you some guidance on how to make the process a lot more enjoyable—or at least less stress inducing!

§ PARTS OF THE APPLICATION

Your law school applications can be found at LSAC.org, the website of the Law School Admissions Council (LSAC). The LSAC's online application system gives you a centralized location through which you can complete and submit multiple applications, thereby sparing you from having to create a separate account on each school's website. The system also records some basic information through the LSAC's Credential Assembly Service (CAS) so that you are not repeatedly entering the same data—you will only need to submit your LSAT, transcripts, and recommendations once. The CAS coordinates and summarizes this information into a standardized format that can then be submitted to all the JD programs to which you are applying. In this way, the CAS basically provides a kind of "back office" service for the law schools, so that they can more efficiently process the applications completed through the LSAC site.

Most JD programs require that candidates submit the following elements to have a completed application, though some small variations may exist from one school to the next:

- A valid LSAT score

- An undergraduate transcript with GPA

- A personal statement (essay)

- Recommendations (typically two to four)

- A résumé

- Basic personal information, including family background, demographic data, etc.

In addition, some law schools will either request or give candidates the opportunity to submit or participate in the following:

- A supplementary statement (essay) or diversity statement

- An addendum or a character and fitness statement

- An in-person or phone interview

§ When to Submit Your Application

You may be surprised to learn that *when* you submit your law school application can actually play a part in your success (or lack thereof) as an applicant. Most schools have what is called "rolling" admissions, which means that once a school's application season starts, the admissions committee accepts applications at any time during that set application season rather than by a specific, predetermined date and begins evaluating the submissions as they are received. As a result, this also means that schools begin *accepting* candidates as soon as applications start to roll in and can be processed. As time passes, then, fewer and fewer spaces remain available in the school's next class. We therefore advise that you strive to submit your application(s) as early in the application cycle as you can without compromising quality. Picture a large auditorium with hundreds of empty seats. Now imagine those seats slowly filling up as a massive line of people works its way in. If you wait too long to enter the auditorium, there may be no seat left for you, no matter how much you might deserve to be in that room. That is the law school admissions process in a nutshell—it gets more and more difficult with each passing day.

THE TRADITIONAL APPLICATION SEASON

Let us take a look at a sample application season schedule to better understand when you should submit your files, at the earliest and at the latest. We hope these examples will allow you to draw parallels with your target schools, though dates will of course differ slightly from one school to another:

- October 1: School begins accepting applications.

- March 15: Last day applications are accepted.

- Mid- to Late April: Most decisions are made by this time.

- May 1: Deposits are due from accepted applicants.

The typical admissions season, as you can see, is fairly straightforward. It begins in the middle of October, so if you were incredibly motivated and had already taken the LSAT in June or earlier, you could be ready to submit your application on day one. Although this kind of immediacy is not crucial, submitting as early as possible—as early as you feel that you have your best application in hand—should be your plan. For any top school, *a mid-November date should be a final personal deadline to target*, whereas December would be "late." Submitting any time after December 20 is basically equivalent to applying in January, given the interruption of the holidays at that time—and January is "really late." Think about that auditorium that is steadily filling—each day, claiming that coveted place in the class becomes more challenging. Admissions seasons pass very quickly and are unforgiving of procrastinators. If you want your best shot at a place in your target school's class, be prepared to get your application in early.

EARLY DECISION AND EARLY ACTION PLANS

Early decision and early action plans are programs through which candidates who have a strong affinity for a particular school can better their chances of acceptance at that school and significantly shorten the length of time they have to wait for a decision by submitting their application by a predetermined date at the very beginning of the application season. Both plans demand that candidates have their applications completed by the outset of the season—which in turn requires careful planning and forethought—and the main difference between the two is that early decision plans involve a binding agreement, whereas early action plans do not. Certain advantages and disadvantages are inherent in each of these types of plans, as we will explain. (Remember, of course, that variations exist from school to school, and that some programs may not offer either of these kinds of plans, so always check directly with your target school for its specific guidelines before preparing to apply.)

Why would law schools offer such plans? One reason is to better understand which candidates truly want to attend their programs, and this knowledge allows the schools to be more judicious with their offers. Candidates who apply early decision *must* enroll if accepted, and those who apply early action are much more likely to enroll, which means that by selecting candidates from these groups, the school will ensure that its "yield"—the ratio of the number of offers given to the number of offers accepted—will be higher. And because rankings factor yield into their school evaluations, schools care about this number, and the better the ratio, the better chance a program has of doing well in the rankings.

Through these plans, schools also ensure that they enroll strong candidates that may have accepted an offer elsewhere if they had applied to many schools during the regular application season. In addition, the plans add a level of efficiency to the selection process, given that the applicants who participate in these plans have already committed to the program or have expressed a particularly strong affinity for it. The admissions committee is therefore not "wasting" time evaluating candidates who really may not be that interested in attending the school.

Early Decision

Applying early decision can confer a kind of "preferred" status on you, but in return, you *must contractually agree* that if you are granted admission, you will not only accept the offer but also withdraw yourself from consideration at any other JD program. As a result, if you are *wholly* committed to a particular school and are prepared and willing to attend it with *no* financial aid, applying in the school's early decision round is a good choice. (Note: We are not saying that you will not receive financial aid if you apply in this round, just that you will need to be prepared to enroll in the school *even if* you are not granted any, given that you will have committed to accepting admission if it is offered, no matter what.) If you are then accepted, you will have plenty of time to address the many matters that go along with attending law school, such as arranging housing, giving notice at your job (if applicable), and preparing to move. On the other hand, should you not be accepted, you are left ample time to apply to other JD programs during the same application season. Submitting an application in a school's early decision round does not mean that you cannot *apply* to other schools, so you can still be conservative and apply to other schools simultaneously, recognizing that those applications could shortly be rendered moot.

The binding aspect of the early decision option means that candidates must be completely certain of their choice. Consider, for example, the following statement from Columbia Law School, which clearly indicates that the top schools share information about applicants in this round to ensure compliance:

Please be aware that, responding to the request of some peer law schools, Columbia will provide these schools with the names of all applicants accepted under our binding Early Decision Plan.

At some schools, applying during the early decision round may require additional application elements, such as an extra essay, so we again encourage you to fully research what your target school's plan requires before deciding on a plan of action.

Early Action

As with early decision plans, early action plans ensure that candidates who apply during this round receive an admissions decision very soon after submitting. Although submitting during this round sends a message to the school that the candidate has an extremely high level of interest in the program, it *does not* involve any kind of binding agreement on the part of the candidate. Early actions plans, therefore, offer the advantage of learning much sooner whether you have secured a spot at your preferred school, but you also retain the option of simultaneously applying to other JD programs and waiting for both acceptance and financial aid decisions from all before determining which to ultimately attend.

§ Components of Your Profile

As was outlined earlier in this chapter, your basic law school application consists of a mixture of statistics (fixed numerical data) and more fluid information about you as an individual, conveyed through such elements as your résumé, personal statement, recommendations, and so on. Law schools evaluate candidates based on, of course, the information provided in the application, with some programs placing more emphasis on certain factors while others weigh different factors more heavily. This next section will try to explain how these various elements are typically processed by the different schools and offer some guidance on how you can evaluate yourself before applying, so as to know whether you can truly be competitive at your target school—and possibly, what is within your power to change before applying (i.e., what you can do to increase your likelihood of being admitted).

§ THE BASIC STATS

Although, as we have noted, your LSAT score(s) and GPA are not the only determining factors in whether you are admitted to your target law school, they do play a crucial role in the schools' decision-making process. Therefore, we will begin by taking a closer look at how these data points are evaluated on the schools' side and how you can determine whether yours measure up.

THE LSAT

When to Take the LSAT

The LSAT is administered four times per year, and the time at which you choose to take it can confer different advantages and disadvantages. Ideally, you should take the LSAT well in advance of the year in which you plan to apply to law school, so that you give yourself ample time to study (most LSAT classes are 12 weeks long) and can thereby alleviate some of the pressure you might otherwise feel if you needed to nail the LSAT right before you submit your applications. Further, if you take the test early, you will have more time to think about school selection and will be able to put together a strong application without worrying about having to take the LSAT at the same time. Because your LSAT score is good for five years, you definitely do not need to wait until the last minute to take the test. However, few people think five years ahead or even a full year ahead of the application season. If you are reading this book as your application season approaches, you should consider the LSAT's four annual test dates and the advantages and disadvantages of each within a single application season.

June

If you take the June LSAT and earn the score you were hoping to achieve, you will be in very good shape for the coming application year. By successfully completing this part of the application process early on, you can close the book on a crucial piece of your application puzzle and start to contemplate the rest of the application. On the other hand, if you do not attain the score you were targeting, you still have time to retake the exam in October. We should note that you should not plan to keep retaking the test until you get your desired score, because you can only take the test three times in a two-year period.

October

Many law school applicants will take the October LSAT, which is the last "early" test for the upcoming application season. You can take the October LSAT and get your scores back within three weeks, which means that you would be able to submit your total application to your target schools in November, a deadline we strongly recommend (we explain why in the next section of this chapter). You might even be able to meet an October application deadline, but your margin for error is minimal. If you do not achieve your desired score on the October LSAT, you can still submit an application and inform the school that you will be retaking the test in December, but that is certainly suboptimal, because spaces in the JD programs are being filled with every day that passes.

December

Taking the LSAT in December is a great idea if you are planning to apply to law school in the following, rather than the current, application season and want to get a head start. However, we do not advise a December date for those who plan to submit an application to a top school in the near term. At this point, you have already passed our suggested November application submission deadline and your target schools will have given many seats away. Taking the LSAT in December also leaves you little or no opportunity to retake the exam, should you not score in your desired range. For many schools, the December LSAT is the *final* test available for the year, so you should consider it only as a last resort. This is not to say that candidates who take the test in December have no chance of gaining admission to their target program—some certainly will—but we strongly recommend that you complete the test earlier and save yourself the added stress, while setting yourself up to be a more competitive candidate.

FEBRUARY

Taking the LSAT in February is really only an option for candidates who plan to apply to law school in the upcoming application season (meaning the coming October), not the current season. Some schools—such as Columbia Law School—will not even accept a candidate's scores from a February test for the current application season. One exception to this guideline, however, might be an otherwise stellar candidate who is very confident that he or she will score exceptionally well on the test and is applying to a school that will still accept the scores. Otherwise, the February test is for the long-term planner, looking to the coming year. If you are just such a candidate, we applaud you!

EVALUATING SCORES

Law school candidates tend to worry about their LSAT score(s) to an inordinate degree, in large part because of what the score seems to imply. Comparing one's LSAT score against the ranges schools post for their most recent classes provides a relatively easy way of "scientifically" gauging one's chances of gaining admission. Indeed, because the test is standardized, such comparisons can imbue an applicant with confidence when his or her score compares favorably, but they can just as easily discourage the applicant when the comparison is less favorable—most importantly, though, in the end, they do not indicate anything *definitive*. Whether a candidate's score is "high enough" is not a cut-and-dry issue—and, of course, some candidates will always feel they could do a little bit better—but scoring within a school's range is a good place to start in establishing a sense of your competitiveness with respect to that program.

Table 1 lists the ranges of scores (as of the writing of this book) at some of the top schools.

Table 1. LSAT 75th–25th Percentile Ranges at a Selection of Top Law Schools

	75th Percentile	25th Percentile
Yale Law School	177	170
Harvard Law School	176	171
Columbia Law School	175	170
New York University School of Law	174	170
University of Chicago Law School	173	167
University of Pennsylvania Law School	171	166
Northwestern Law	171	165
University of Virginia School of Law	171	165
Duke University School of Law	171	167
University of Michigan Law School	170	167
University of California, Berkeley, School of Law	169	164
Cornell Law School	169	166

Source: Data retrieved from each school's website in February 2012.

This table presents the 75th to 25th percentile ranges for the LSAT for a selection of schools, meaning that any applicant who has an LSAT score that falls within this range for a given school effectively has a score on par with the "middle" of that school's most recent class (i.e., the 50% of students who scored higher than the lowest scoring 25% of the class yet lower than the highest scoring 25% of the class). As you assess your candidacy, you can start by checking your target school's LSAT score range and seeing whether you fit within the middle 50% of its class. If you find that your score is at the lower end of the range, remember that 25% of the school's class had scores that fell *below* this range. This means that you should not immediately assume that you will be rejected by the school based on your score alone, because obviously, other candidates with scores below this range were accepted. Of course, if your score is outside this middle 50% range, the onus is on you to prove that you possess other, intangible qualities that will allow you to prove yourself and that will make you a strong law school student who can contribute to the school's community. If you find that you are in the top 25%, this is not a reason to be cocky or to take for granted that you will be accepted. If the rest of your application is not strong enough or you do not present your candidacy properly, you could still knock yourself out of contention!

The administrators of the LSAT release raw scores and percentile scores that reveal how candidates have performed relative to the entire pool of LSAT test takers.

Table 2. LSAT Scores and Percentiles

Scaled Score	Percentile
180	99th
175	99th
170	98th
165	93rd
160	82nd
150	45th
140	13th
130	2nd
120	0

Source: Manhattan LSAT

By comparing the percentiles in Table 2 with the score ranges in Table 1, you will see that students in the bottom portion (25%) of Yale Law School's range scored a 170 overall—the bottom of Yale's range is still ranked among those who score a 98th percentile score! Just to be clear, this would mean that only 1 of 100 overall test-takers will perform better than those who rate at the

25th percentile of Yale's class. Meanwhile, the bottom portion of the Berkeley School of Law range (those with scores equal to 164) ranks in roughly the 93rd percentile, meaning that 6 of 100 overall LSAT-takers will perform better than those at this "low" indicator. If you find the high scores necessary to fall into just the bottom of these ranges daunting, take a moment to consider Yale's full LSAT range, as reported on its site for the Class of 2014: although the highest score is an intimidating 180, the lowest score is a notably imperfect 157. Granted, judging by this information, the applicant who gains admission to Yale with a 157 LSAT score must be a very special individual with a lot to offer in the other areas of his or her candidacy.

Given these LSAT ranges, the competition is undoubtedly intense at the top schools, so performing well on the LSAT is clearly a crucial part of an applicant's candidacy. Of course, test days do not always go as planned, so you may be wondering what happens if you crack under pressure while taking the test, or whether you can or should retake the test if you do not attain your target score the first time.

First, if after taking the LSAT, you truly believe that you performed much worse than you could have and that your final score will be a notably inaccurate representation of your abilities, you *can* cancel your score within six days of taking the test. However, this option is not meant to be an "easy out." Try not to second-guess yourself; very likely, you should only consider canceling your score if you omitted a significant number of answers or believe you may have made mistakes when rushing to fill in responses at the end of the test, or if a larger issue—such as illness—prevented you from performing at your usual level. You do not want to make a hasty or overcautious decision and cancel a perfectly good score. Nonetheless, be assured that if you choose to cancel your score once, this will not reflect badly on you as an applicant. These things happen, and admissions officers understand that people have off days. What about canceling twice? Well, if you do quite well the third time you take the test, having two previous cancellations should not really matter, but you may start to run the risk of sending the wrong message about your ability to manage stress.

And canceling your score three times may send an even louder message about your frame of mind—and it will also prevent you from taking the test again for two years, as we noted earlier. We hate to put pressure on you, but three times better be a charm.

Ideally, of course, you will take the test once and it will go well for you. However, if things do not work out that way, you need not worry that an admissions officer will refuse to forgive a second test. Many admissions officers have rankings in the back of their minds at all times and would like to be able to report the highest possible average LSAT scores to *U.S. News & World Report* and other organizations that publish rankings surveys. So, motivated by this upside, most will give consideration to your highest score, even if they say otherwise or make vague, noncommittal comments on this point on the school's website. A well-placed source told jdMission of these policies, "Anyone who says that they are averaging LSAT scores down is full of it."

Our friends at Manhattan LSAT have researched these policies and categorized schools according to how they claim to assess candidates' LSAT scores, as follows:

Accept Applicant's Highest LSAT Score

Cornell University Law School

Northwestern University Law School

University of California, Berkeley, School of Law

University of Chicago Law School

University of Michigan Law School

University of Virginia School of Law

Accept Applicant's Average LSAT Score

Duke University School of Law

New York University School of Law

Examine All LSAT Scores

Columbia Law School

Harvard Law School

University of Pennsylvania Law School

Yale Law School

Some schools obviously say they examine and evaluate all the LSAT scores submitted by an applicant; although these schools will still consider an individual's highest score, they will examine all the data to see whether they can identify any aberrations or trends that may require further examination or that may shed more light on the candidate's capabilities. For example, a big leap in an applicant's score from his or her initial test to the second may validate the applicant's claim of having had an "off" first test day. A few other schools claim to average candidates' scores, but all such claims should be taken with a grain of salt. In addition, policies change, so check with your target schools individually to determine the current standing of their policies.

Of course, your LSAT score does not stand alone in your application. Your GPA works in concert with your LSAT score to tell the admissions committee whether you can handle law school's rigorous curriculum. These metrics are evaluated in tandem, with different schools placing different emphasis on each metric.

YOUR GPA

In Table 3, we present the 75th to 25th percentile ranges for average GPAs at the top law schools. You will see that the GPA numbers at these schools are — not surprisingly—often quite high.

Table 3. 75th–25th Percentile GPA Ranges at a Selection of Top Law Schools

	75th GPA	25th GPA
Harvard Law School	3.97	3.78
Yale Law School	3.96	3.83
University of Chicago Law School	3.94	3.71
University of Virginia School of Law	3.94	3.49
University of Pennsylvania Law School	3.93	3.58
New York University School of Law	3.90	3.60
Northwestern University Law School	3.90	3.40
University of California, Berkeley, School of Law	3.88	3.62
University of Michigan Law School	3.87	3.59
Duke University School of Law	3.84	3.62
Columbia Law School	3.82	3.60
Cornell Law School	3.77	3.51

Source: Data retrieved from each school's website in February 2012.

Again, as you gauge the strength of your candidacy at your target school(s), you will want to get a sense of where you fall within its GPA range. If your GPA falls in the middle of your school's range, you are likely in a comfortable place statistically. That said, admissions committees will go beyond the absolute number itself to consider the difficulty of your degree and the trends within your transcript. For example, you may not know that a 4.0 GPA in engineering is virtually unheard of. The admissions officers, however, are well aware of this fact and will therefore understand that a 3.75 in this field is remarkable and a 3.5 GPA is still strong. (Further, to avoid any bias created by grade inflation, they will also check your class rank to better gauge your academic strength.)

Meanwhile, if, for example, you graduated with a 3.4 GPA in art history, but you had an awful freshman year in which you had a 2.4 but then earned a 3.75 GPA each year thereafter, the schools will take your improvement and progression into account. In addition, we should note that admissions officers are interested in composing a diverse class of incoming students, so the applicant with the engineering degree and the one with a specialization in art history are actually on even footing to start—you do not need to have been "pre-law" to get into law school. Try to think of the admissions officer as a kind of detective—he or she is trying to read your transcript on a deeper level to discover the broader story of your academic experience and to thereby determine whether you have the necessary skills, experience, and character to join the class.

International candidates might worry that an admissions committee will not understand their undergrad school's grading system, but we can assure you that the admissions officers have definitely seen it all. You can be confident that your target school will know how to interpret your grades on a comparative level, whether you have a percentage score from a Canadian school or a rating on a 12-point scale from an institution in Ukraine.

Some applicants also erroneously believe that their undergraduate school's ranking and reputation will dramatically affect their chances for admission. After all, the elite law schools want students from elite undergrad schools, right? Yale Law wants Yale grads, right? And they would never accept a candidate from a school that does not ooze prestige, right? Wrong. Elite schools want *elite individuals*, and such individuals could have graduated from literally *any* undergraduate institution. Let us use Harvard Law School's 2010–2011 student body as an illustration. The diversity of schools these students are from might surprise you. Two-hundred sixty-one undergraduate colleges are represented among its almost 600 students, including this random selection of six colleges (collected with the swipe of a mouse, thus the alphabetical order):

- Ner Israel Rabbinical College
- New England Conservatory of Music
- The New School
- University of Waterloo
- University of Western Ontario

- University of Wisconsin–Eau Claire

Playing the same game with Yale Law's list of the 74 schools represented among the roughly 214 students in its Class of 2014, we selected these six schools (via mouse) at random:

- Purdue University–West Lafayette
- Reed College
- Saint Peter's College
- Samford University
- Scripps College
- Seoul National University

Clearly, a true diversity of undergraduate institutions is typically represented at top law schools. And one thing that should be obvious is that you cannot go back in time and change your alma mater, so stop worrying about your undergraduate institution and focus instead on your performance or, if you did not do well, the positive trends that may be found therein.

HOW THESE NUMBERS ARE EVALUATED

Although we stand behind our assertion that schools do not view candidates' profiles purely scientifically, we do need to admit that some science can come into play in the admissions process. To illustrate, we first ask you which of the following candidates you would rather be, if you could choose:

	LSAT Score	GPA
Candidate 1	180	3.30
Candidate 2	175	3.50
Candidate 3	170	3.70

The truth is, there is no definitively "right" answer. You may be surprised to learn that none of these candidates is necessarily "better" than the others based on these numbers alone (for our purposes here, we will ignore the rest of these applicants' stories). Whether these combinations of GPA and LSAT score would prove advantageous at a particular school depends entirely on the school in question. Many law schools actually use special equations to create a harmonized score for each candidate using his or her LSAT score and GPA. In doing so, the schools have created a way to measure the combined value of these metrics. (The schools even publish these equations. Create an account with LSAC and then within your home page, find "transcripts" and on that page find "admissions index." There you will find all the equations!)

Now, do not get carried away thinking you have found the key to determining your chances at your target school. Although the programs publish these equations, they offer no guidance as to what the outputs mean. You can calculate your own aggregate score by inserting your LSAT score and GPA into the equations, of course, but you will not be able to know how your target school would view your aggregate score, in other words, whether it would be considered "good" or not. We believe these equations do reveal one thing, though—whether a school has a slight bias toward the GPA or the LSAT.

As examples, let us take a look at Berkeley Law's and Stanford Law School's equations:

School	Candidate's LSAT score multiplied by	+	Candidate's GPA multiplied by	+/−	Constant
University of California, Berkeley, School of Law	0.871	+	23.487	+	8.474
Stanford Law School	0.018	+	0.402	+	−1.172

On their own, these figures probably mean nothing to you, so to illuminate better how this works, let us run the equations for Candidates 1, 2, and 3, who we introduced earlier, using Berkeley Law's equation ([Candidate's LSAT score × 0.871] + [Candidate's GPA × 23.487] + 8.474 = Aggregate):

	LSAT	GPA	Constant	Aggregate	Rank
Candidate 1	180	3.30	8.474	242.8	3
Candidate 2	175	3.50	8.474	243.1	2
Candidate 3	170	3.70	8.474	243.4	1

Using Berkeley Law's equation, Candidate 3, who has a 170 LSAT score and a 3.70 GPA, has the best composite ranking. Meanwhile, running the exact same numbers through Stanford Law's equation ([Candidate's LSAT score × 0.018] + [Candidate's GPA × 0.402] + [−1.172] = Aggregate) yields very different results:

	LSAT	GPA	Constant	Aggregate	Rank
Candidate 1	180	3.30	−1.172	3.395	1
Candidate 2	175	3.50	−1.172	3.385	2
Candidate 3	170	3.70	−1.172	3.375	3

At Stanford Law, Candidate 1 would be ranked first, though this same candidate ranked third when the numbers were run through Berkeley Law's equation—and vice versa. So what do these outputs tell us? They reveal that on a relative basis, Berkeley Law places more emphasis on a candidate's GPA, and Stanford Law places more emphasis on a candidate's LSAT score. What is especially interesting is that the individual with the perfect LSAT score, Candidate 1, is the lowest ranked using Berkeley Law's equation. Although he or she may still have a very strong application overall and a very high—and thus very helpful—LSAT score, this simple exercise demonstrates that one's LSAT score is not everything.

How can you use this information to your advantage, then? If you happen to have a high LSAT score but a low GPA, or a low LSAT score but a high GPA, you can use these equations to identify schools that favor your strengths. Still, you should not be deluded into thinking that a high GPA and terrible LSAT score will get you into a school like Berkeley Law, which values candidates' GPAs more highly. These *relative* weightings are not capable of turning a weak candidate into a strong one! You might view the information these equations produce as providing a little nudge in one direction or the other as you consider different schools. That said, make sure that you are applying to JD programs that truly interest you and offer the resources you need, not schools that simply have favorable equations. (Please see Appendix A for a more thorough explanation of the relative value of GPAs and LSAT scores at certain law schools.)

To sum up, as a candidate, you can consult your target school's GPA and LSAT score 75th–25th percentile ranges to gain a broad understanding of where you might stand at the very beginning of the race. Your scores will place you into one of the following five categories:

1. High GPA and high LSAT score: Your place in the class is most likely yours to lose.

2. Middle LSAT score and middle GPA: You are in the hunt but will have to put together a compelling application package.

3. High GPA and low LSAT score: You are in the hunt but will have to put together a compelling application package.

4. High LSAT score and low GPA: You are in the hunt but will have to put together a compelling application package.

5. Low LSAT score and low GPA: You will need an extraordinarily strong story and application to succeed.

Beyond the Numbers

Law school admissions officers go to great lengths to persuade applicants that their candidacies are more than the simple sum of their GPA and LSAT scores, because they worry that otherwise well-qualified candidates may feel that they do not measure up statistically and will decide not to apply. We are not suggesting that schools are seeking candidates with mediocre grades and LSAT scores, but candidates with lower than average scores *can* succeed. After all, the nature of an average is such that some people are above it and others are below it—and the schools ask for qualitative data (résumés, essays, etc.) for a reason, which is to get to know the individual behind the stats.

So this is the point when many of you may roll your eyes and want to dismiss what we are saying because you have heard so many stories about and from individuals who were accepted at every school to which they applied, "just because" of their GPA or LSAT result and nothing else. If you do not believe us, consider what the associate dean of admissions at what is arguably the most prestigious and selective law school in the world—Yale Law School (YLS)—has to say on the matter. Asha Rangappa has consistently gone on the record to declare that the issue of law school application statistics is overblown. She told Top-Law-Schools.com:

> *The biggest misconception is that we base our admission on numbers alone. I am amazed that this misconception persists.... We have too few spots to just bring in the people who happened to score well on exams and standardized tests. We use these numbers to be confident in an applicant's academic potential—we don't want to bring someone here who can't handle the work and will struggle—but beyond that we want people who are interesting, multifaceted, intellectually curious, and will be great lawyers and representatives of YLS. Numbers don't tell you about these things.*[1]

On her entertaining and freewheeling blog, Rangappa expanded on her "scores are not everything" contention, stating that applicants should not be asking, "Can you get in with low scores?" but rather, "Why are you rejecting so many people with high scores?"

---

1 "Interview with Asha Rangappa, Associate Dean of Yale Law School," Top-Law-Schools.com, accessed February 2012, www.top-law-schools.com/asha-rangappa-interview.html.

As I've mentioned before, a weak number does usually need extremely strong everything else to make it through to the faculty, which is why I have to read through the whole thing [the application], including the recommendations. Actually, a better topic for discussion might be what would keep someone with really strong numbers from being passed on... which happens with surprising frequency.[2]

If you go looking, you will find plenty of blog posts, interviews, and other instances in which law school admissions directors attempt to dispel the myth that the GPA/LSAT score combination is all that matters. So, a question is begged, what else are the schools evaluating?

Basically, after scrutinizing your scores to first ensure that you can manage the work law school requires, the admissions committee will turn to your résumé, recommendations, personal statement, and, if provided, optional diversity essay, and may possibly even interview you to better understand your interests and motivations—all to get a more rounded sense of you as a person. Essentially, the entire application presents an opportunity for you to tell your story. Even though candidates with a high GPA and/or a stellar LSAT score will grab the admissions committee's attention, these applicants still need well-rounded, compelling stories to really get the door to swing open. Other candidates may have stories that are interesting enough to get them to the doorstep, and their scores are *just* sufficient to open the door. These two aspects of your profile—your statistics and the nonquantifiable elements of your candidacy—work together to make an impression on the admissions officers, so you should not pin your hopes on just one or the other.

---

2 Asha Rangappa, "Your Burning Questions Answered," *(203) Admissions Blog*, Yale Law School, February 12, 2010, http://blogs.law.yale.edu/blogs/admissions/archive/2010/02/12/your-burning-questions-answered.aspx.

§ The Nonquantifiable Components of Your Candidacy

In short, the nonquantifiable aspects of your candidacy are those elements of your character that cannot be measured easily (or at all) on a numerical scale—things like ambition, creativity, compassion, humor, and charisma. These components make up your personality, the essence of *who you are as an individual*, and these in turn have been shaped by your life experiences and background. Through your résumé, essays, recommendations, interview, and other non-numbers-based portions of your application, you have the opportunity to convey these aspects of your character to the admissions committees so they can gain an understanding of you as a whole person and can better determine whether you would be a good fit with their program.

Sharing the story of the life you live—and have lived—helps paint a more complete picture of the person you are. People tend to seek out opportunities and responsibilities that speak to them, that match their values and/or fulfill an interest, so what you have spent your time doing and the choices you have made along the way send a message to others about what is important to you and what you are capable of. As an illustration, consider a theatrical presentation—some candidates might be drawn to a behind-the-scenes technical role, others would want to play the main character on center stage, while still others would opt for a directorial position, and yet others may prefer to work at advertising and promoting the production. The kinds of roles and responsibilities people choose for themselves speak volumes about the kind of person they are and how they interact with the world around them, and this is extremely valuable information for an admissions committee.

Your job as an applicant is therefore to use the various parts of your application to ensure that you convey a complete impression of yourself to your target school. A logical question, then, would be: What qualities and experiences do the top programs want to see? Do they want the kind of candidates who would pursue the "behind-the-scenes technical" role, the "main character" role or the "director" role? Indeed, there is no prototypical law school candidate. Let us consider, for example, characteristics from YLS's Class of 2014. All the following statistics are true about these students, seeming at first glance to imply a bias of some kind on the school's part for candidates with these characteristics:

- The students' average age is 24 years old.

- A full 45% of the class is one to two years out of college.

- Students of color make up 38% of the class.[3]

More importantly, however, the following facts are also true, demonstrating just how different these individuals are and what a wide range of life experiences they represent:

- Students have worked or lived in 71 different countries around the world.

- Students can speak and/or read almost 40 different languages.

- Students have undergraduate degrees from more than 70 different institutions.

- Individuals in the class include a deckhand on a fishing boat, a kickboxing champion, governmental policy advisors, a concert violinist, triathletes and marathoners, a tournament Scrabble player, an insurance adjuster, and a parachuting coach.[4]

Avoid consulting a school's class profile and assuming that because a certain group is well represented, you must also fit into that group to succeed. Success actually lies in effectively conveying the most important parts of your profile that are unique to you.

---

3   Entering Class Profile, Yale Law School website, accessed February 24, 2012, www.law.yale.edu/admissions/profile.htm.
4   Entering Class Profile, Yale Law School website, accessed February 24, 2012, www.law.yale.edu/admissions/profile.htm.

Law schools go to great lengths in fact to dismiss the idea of "the perfect candidate." Thus, if you are applying to law school in the short term, think about the elements of yourself that you want to convey—ideally focusing on elements that are not easily categorizable—and then identify experiences and stories from your life that best illustrate them. If you plan to apply to law school at some future date, seek out opportunities in the meantime that you can later use to illustrate the interests, abilities, and other aspects of yourself you will want the admissions committees to understand. You will need to push yourself in the applicable academic, professional, community, and personal spheres and make the most of all opportunities before you.

We have already established that top law schools receive applications from more great candidates than they can accept, and they offer admission to some candidates who do not have sky-high LSAT scores or GPAs. Stop for a moment and put yourself in the shoes of someone on the admissions committee. You see one candidate with a 3.65 GPA who studied diligently throughout college but was otherwise uninvolved, and another with a 3.60 GPA who was a research assistant and got his or her name on a publication while in college. Which applicant would you assume had more drive and ambition? That additional .05 GPA should not speak as loudly in the first candidate's favor as the research publication—which is a more unique achievement—would in the second's. Most decisions are not as simple as this, though, and admissions officers are not often gauging candidates who are "apples to apples" other than a mere .05 GPA difference and a published paper, of course. However, when admissions officers see overwhelming and consistent evidence of drive, character, and excellence with relation to the following kinds of activities, it sends a strong positive message:

- Academics, in the form of research, teaching assistantships, independent study, publications, scholarships, awards, etc.

- Student leadership, in the form of student club offices, student government positions, campus newspaper involvement, student athletics, etc.

- Community endeavors, in the form of volunteer work, social/political involvement, etc.

- Work experience, in the form of paying your way through school, earning rapid promotions, achieving specific project-related goals, gaining profound experience in a unique field, etc.

- Personal accomplishments, in the form of a commitment to athletics, languages, the arts, entrepreneurship, etc.

Pinning down exactly what you "should" have accomplished in these areas (or should do in the future, if you are not applying to law school right away) to ensure that you are an interesting person is extremely difficult—and most candidates will not have good stories to tell in *all* of these categories. However, a successful individual will draw upon these kinds of experiences to produce a standout résumé, recommendation, personal statement, and possibly interview. And as a result, he or she will naturally make an impression on the admissions committee. Again, you cannot artificially manufacture these experiences, and the schools cannot definitively say that they are more interested in candidates with one kind of background over another—a volunteer firefighter rather than a volunteer emergency medical technician, for example, or a science teacher rather than a scientist or an individual with an advanced degree in the sciences. Your choices and accomplishments related to these kinds of pursuits are what will tell the story of who you are.

You may want to believe that there is a clear path or recipe for success, but the only real key is to be as genuine and thorough as possible in sharing the parts of your background and character that best display your individuality. Sometimes applicants get carried away with thinking that the number of activities they can claim is what will impress the admissions committee, but admissions officers are interested in *quality* of activity, not quantity—they care about impact, not titles.

CHAPTER 2

GRABBING THEIR ATTENTION VIA YOUR PERSONAL STATEMENT

We would guess that you are most likely not looking forward to writing your law school application essay, but you should actually view this chance to submit a personal statement as a gift from the admissions committees—they are giving you the opportunity to tell them absolutely anything you want about yourself. For some candidates, this assignment may be daunting at first—after all, where do you begin? With some time and reflection, though, you should be able to seize this opportunity and use it to fundamentally shape the admissions committees' perspective of you as a candidate. At this point in the application process, you have limited control over most of the components of your candidacy—your GPA was determined years ago, for example, and your recommendations are in someone else's hands. Yet what you present in your personal statement—and how—is completely up to you, so think carefully about the best way you can represent yourself. In this chapter, we offer guidance, advice, and ideas to help you in writing your personal statement and, we hope, to provide some inspiration as well.

§ Types of Essays

Law school applicants are typically responsible for writing one or more of the following three kinds of application essays: a traditional personal statement, a free-form essay, and an optional diversity essay. Which one(s) you will write depends on the school or schools to which you are applying and the story you wish to tell the admissions committee about yourself. In this section, we will describe (and offer examples of) the different kinds of essays law schools want and discuss various ways of making your writing more compelling and effective.

Here we have assembled a sampling of the kinds of essay questions you will encounter when working on your law school applications. We have extracted these from some top law programs' past applications (please note that we have sometimes abbreviated the schools' directions):

Please provide more information about yourself in a written personal state-ment. The subject matter of the essay is up to you, but keep in mind that the reader will be seeking a sense of you as a person and as a potential student and graduate of Berkeley Law.

—Berkeley School of Law

Please use the personal statement to introduce yourself to the admissions committee and to help the committee get to know you on a personal level. It should demonstrate your contribution to the law school community beyond simply academics. The admissions committee generally finds that a state-ment that focuses on a unique personal attribute or experience is usually the most informative (as opposed to a restatement of your qualifications or résumé).

—University of Chicago Law School

Candidates to Columbia Law School are required to submit a personal essay or statement supplementing required application materials. Such a statement may provide the admissions committee with information regard-ing such matters as: personal, family, or educational background; experi-ences and talents of special interest; reasons for applying to law school as they may relate to personal goals and professional expectations; or any other factors that you think should inform the committee's evaluation of your candidacy for admission.

—Columbia Law School

The personal statement is intended as an opportunity to give the admis-sions committee a better sense of who you are as a person and as a potential student and graduate of Harvard Law School. In many instances, appli-cants have used the personal statement to provide more context on how their experiences and strengths could make them valuable contributors to the Harvard and legal communities, to illuminate their intellectual back-

ground and interests, or to clarify or elaborate on other information in their application. Because applicants and their experiences differ, you are the best person to determine the content of your statement.

—Harvard Law School

A. Personal Statement (required): There is no formula for a successful personal statement, and different individuals will find different topics to be well-suited to them. Applicants have, for example, elaborated on their significant life experiences; meaningful intellectual interests and extracurricular activities; factors inspiring them to obtain a legal education or to pursue particular career goals....

—The University of Michigan Law Schsool

The admissions committee requires that every applicant submit an original example of written expression. The purpose of this personal statement is to provide you with as flexible an opportunity as possible to submit information that you deem important to your candidacy. You may wish to describe aspects of your background and interests—intellectual, personal, or professional—and how you will uniquely contribute to the Penn Law community and/or the legal profession.

—The University of Pennsylvania Law School

You will note that all of these essay questions use the phrase "personal statement." Traditionally, "personal statement" has specifically referred to an essay in which a candidate explains why he or she wishes to earn a JD and describes his or her relevant life experiences. These days, however, a "personal statement" can be any essay that discusses something important to or about the applicant that the applicant wishes to share with the admissions committee. This means that in response to your target school's essay question, you can write either a *traditional* personal statement or what we call a free-form essay. (We discuss the optional diversity essay in detail later in this section, and Chapter 4, "Making the Most of Addenda," offers an in-depth explanation of addenda, which are shorter essays generally used to address "issues" in one's candidacy.)

§ THE TRADITIONAL PERSONAL STATEMENT

As noted earlier, in a *traditional* personal statement, you explicitly demonstrate a connection between your past experiences and your current interest in attending law school. This kind of essay is a great deal more straightforward than the free-form essay, though it is not necessarily easier to write. Effectively communicating to the admissions committee why you want to go to law school requires a good deal of self-awareness and self-study. Career changers in particular have to make truly convincing and reasoned arguments about their decision to pursue a law degree. What brings about self-awareness and facilitates self-study? Research, research, research. This includes visiting law schools, sitting in on classes, speaking with law professors and students, visiting the schools' career services offices, and/or possibly even working for a time in the legal profession. We do not recommend that you write about what you want to do in your legal career—or possibly even pursue one—if what you want to achieve in your life does not in fact require a law degree. Fully investigating your target JD programs and identifying clear connections between the resources they offer and what you have already accomplished in your life, in addition to what you hope to do in the future, is a crucial part of successfully writing this kind of essay.

If you choose to write a traditional personal statement, your essay must convince the admissions committee that attending law school is the logical—if not necessary—next step in your life's pursuit. For example, a social worker citing frustrations with the foster care system could make a convincing argument for wanting to work in the field of juvenile law. In the following sample traditional personal statement, the author convincingly demonstrates why she would ultimately like to work for a legal defense fund.

SAMPLE TRADITIONAL PERSONAL STATEMENT

Before anything, I am B.K. Lingagowder's granddaughter. This may mean nothing to someone outside my family, but it means everything to me. I am also a Badaga, part of a disappearing indigenous tribe from India, yet I am an American as well, having been born in Brooklyn. I lived in India with my grandfather until I was six and then spent three months of every year there with him until I was 21.

He was my moral compass. A village elder for our tribe, he led by example. People sought him out to discuss familial disputes or other tribal controversies. As a member of the Legislative Assembly of India, he strove to raise awareness of the plight of the Badagas, discriminated against as a backward or scheduled caste. He wore exclusively homespun fabric, showing his pride at being a member of the National Party and welcoming dignitaries such as Jawaharlal Nehru and Indira Gandhi to our ancestral home. Our talks as we walked through his tea fields were often about how my duty would be to always uphold the Lingagowder name and serve my family, my community, and my country. When my grandfather died, I felt lost.

I had just graduated from Princeton's Woodrow Wilson School of Public and International Affairs. I was debating my next steps and thought my calling might be in government, as my grandfather's had been. Soon after, I won a scholarship to work for a congressman in Washington, DC, as a liaison between his office and the Indian-American community. At the time, I had only just become comfortable with my hybrid identity as an Indian American. For many years, I had felt like a stranger in both America and India, not feeling that I truly belonged in either country. At Princeton, surrounded by intelligent and worldly classmates, I had finally learned about and embraced my unique cultural role.

Congress was a most unwelcome shock. I had never met so many people who knew so little about someone like me. Very few could even find India on the map. Being Indian American was easily confused with being Native American. No one appeared concerned about what being an Indian American in America really means. Nevertheless, I did not condemn the politicians around me for their oversights. I believe that as a community, Indian Americans have an obligation to educate themselves about U.S. legal and political processes and to become part of the country's social and political fabric. So, I created a political education organization—the National Association of Indian Americans—calling on all first- and second-generation Indian Americans to invest in their future and in that of their children.

That I felt a desire to learn more about the legal system is only natural, I suppose, and I started to think seriously about going to law school. I knew that I no longer wanted to be a political representative or diplomat. Instead, I wanted to study the Indian-American experience from a legal perspective, looking particularly at the group's exclusion from legal and political participation. Patricia J. Williams's book The Alchemy of Race and Rights: Diary of a Law Professor *introduced me to critical race theory. I was truly inspired. A year later, I had the privilege of sitting in on one of Williams's classes at Columbia University, and it was one of the most invigorating classroom experiences I have ever had. Students were heatedly debating the merits of examining everyday interactions and finding the racial component in them as a means of moving the racial equality cause forward. I knew immediately that I wanted to be part of such a dynamic educational community, and as soon as I returned home, I began studying for the LSAT and making preparations to apply to Columbia Law School. That classroom experience solidified for me that a legal education and degree will best equip me to be effective in my chosen career.*

I ultimately see myself working at a legal defense fund, helping promote civil rights through litigation, advocacy, education, and organizing. In this respect, Columbia Law School's Human Rights Clinic will be an ideal practical complement to my educational and intellectual experience, facilitating hands-on practice, with particularly remarkable international opportunities, which will be crucial as I transition into my legal career. I also believe the research and opportunities sponsored by the Center for Intersectionality and Social Policy Studies relate directly to my area of interest and will expose me to valuable new concepts, issues, and strategies. With a law degree, I could provide assistance to the poor and to civil rights and voting rights activists, and bring lawsuits against violators of civil rights. I feel that in many ways, this road was paved for me, yet in other ways, I have paved it for and by myself. In the end, I hope to follow my grandfather's model of serving others and to ultimately make him—wherever he may be—as proud of me as I have always been of him. That would put a smile on my face.

In this essay, the candidate demonstrates a very clear connection between both her past experience and her personal identity and her desire to attend law school. After finding her calling while on Capitol Hill, she knows she *needs* a law degree to become the champion/advocate she now longs to be. She is indeed on a personal mission, and law school is that vital bridge between where she now is and where she wants to go in the future. Further, she makes her claim even more compelling by connecting her desire for a JD with Columbia Law School specifically, by describing her connection to Professor Williams, detailing her classroom experience, and referencing the school's Human Rights Clinic and the Center for Intersectionality and Social Policy Studies. Her essay therefore does not just send the message "I must go to law school," but says, "I must go to *Columbia Law School*," which will have a much stronger impact on the admissions officer who will ultimately read this candidate's file.

§ THE FREE-FORM ESSAY

The free-form essay allows the law school admissions committee to learn more about you as a person, aside from your career path thus far and your aspirations to attend law school. The committee basically wants to know whether you are, first, likeable, and, second, interesting; in other words, will your potential future classmates enjoy seeing you in class, and do you bring any unique elements to the classroom and the school as a whole? This is not the time to reiterate what the admissions committee already knows about you from the other portions of your application, particularly your résumé and your recommendations. Instead, this essay is your chance to "wow" your admissions reader with a uniquely personal and passionate story that will convince him or her that you possess qualities that would make you an asset to the incoming law school class. Understandably, candidates tend to worry about making the "right" topic choice for this essay, because the questions are often so open-ended, but if you carefully think about the impression you want to make and feel that what you have written provides this impression to the best of your ability, and reveals depth of character, you are probably on the right path.

In the following sample free-form essay, the writer describes his passion for soccer and the way he used that passion to change the lives of some teenagers born to poor Colombian immigrants in America.

SAMPLE FREE-FORM ESSAY

"GOOOOOOOL! GOL! GOL! GOL!" Every day for two years, at exactly 4:00 a.m., my father would wake me with this unique alarm, so that I would be on time for my morning soccer drills with America de Cali, a professional soccer team in Colombia with whom I had the privilege of training when I was young. Although my dreams of playing professionally ended after I later suffered a serious knee injury, I continued to play for the joy of the game, the companionship and the pride it brought, and I was fortunate to share these benefits with the teenage children of Colombian immigrants I met when I first arrived in the United States.

Growing up, my friends and I imagined the United States as a place where anything and everything fortuitous could happen to us immediately upon arrival. When, at the age of 25, I first visited my aunts and their families in Union City, New Jersey, however, very little in their lives resembled the images from my youthful imagination of what life in America was supposed to be like. Instead of the big, beautiful houses we had conjured in our dreams, their "houses" were actually just single rooms, each one occupied by a large family, with all the families sharing cramped amenities. My relatives worked long hours just to pay the bills, and my cousins rarely left their apartments, let alone Union City. I understood struggle, having experienced it firsthand, but I could not accept the despondency and defeat I saw in the eyes of my aunts, their family members, and their neighbors. I wanted to give my cousins and their friends, who were also the children of immigrants, a window into a different world, and I did so using—of all things—a mere soccer ball. A quick pick-up game with my cousins slowly turned into weekly lessons/practices with them and a group of their peers, and they would regularly play late into the night. With America de Cali, I had learned how to run clinics that were practical yet fun, and I was able to use these skills to coach my cousins and their friends. In time, I began to see a new light in these young people's eyes.

The teenagers I found myself coaching had grown up immersed in U.S. culture—they were fans of American football and rooted for the New York Giants, they barely spoke their native Spanish, and for them, soccer was but a newborn pastime in the United States. Their interests and experience in America thus far had created a separation between them and their parents, who did not share the teenagers' appreciation for American football and lamented the loss of a connection with their children that the language barrier had caused. However, as they watched their children learn and develop a passion for the sport of their youth, this gap began to close. My insistence that we all speak only Spanish during practice aided this process. We also "adopted" a soccer team from Pereira, Colombia—my hometown—and followed its games enthusiastically throughout the season. These games not only allowed me to point out complex soccer moves in action but also reinforced the teenagers' connection to their native language and their roots in Colombia. As a result, the kids gained a sense of belonging to something larger than their isolated immigrant community in Union City. Once this *initial connection was established, I was able to also teach them about Pereira's remarkable coffee culture, about Colombia's distinguished heritage, and about their own great cultural inheritance. I now saw pride in their faces—pride in themselves and in their community.*

As the soccer season drew to a close, our weekly games were soon replaced by fiestas each weekend at a different player's home, and everyone was invited. To the sounds of vallenatos *(traditional music of Colombia), we ate* arepa de choclo *(corn cakes),* sopa de sancocho *(chicken stew), and, our favorite,* chocolate con pan *(bread soaked in homemade chocolate). During these parties, the older teenagers, many of whom were ready for their first full-time job, would talk about their aspirations for the future. These conversations sometimes led to informal internships with my friends and acquaintances in New York City that I helped arrange. For example, one of the players went to work for a friend of mine from Brazil who had just started an event planning company in midtown Manhattan. Another came to work for my wife in her family's restaurant so he could learn about restaurant management. These young people's eyes were opened to the wonderfully vibrant city in their backyard as well as to the innumerable and exciting opportunities it offered.*

These kids' fervor for soccer led them to embrace their hyphenated identities, to be proud U.S. citizens of Latin American descent. This in turn gave them the confidence to strive for more in their lives in this country and set the stage for future success. As any soccer player will attest, true magic can be found in the spin of a soccer ball.

Note that in this essay, no explicit connection is made between the life experience the candidate describes and his desire or need to attend law school. In fact, the words "law school" do not appear even once in this essay. Why, then, is this an effective response to the law school's essay question? In addition to being well written and engaging, it illustrates that the candidate has profound values—he is clearly committed to his countrymen, his heritage, and his new community. Moreover, he demonstrates that he is motivated and enterprising in creating a stronger sense of community and generating opportunity for others. This indicates that he has strong leadership qualities and possibly even some entrepreneurial tendencies. The slow but steady revelation of the teenagers' transformation holds the reader's attention, which implies that this candidate is interesting and has unique stories to tell. These are all appealing qualities to a law school admissions committee.

§ THE OPTIONAL DIVERSITY ESSAY

In addition to a personal statement, most law schools invite applicants to highlight a unique aspect of their profile via an optional diversity essay. As one example, Stanford Law School includes the following instructions in its application materials:

> *If you would like the committee to consider how factors such as your background, life and work experiences, advanced studies, extracurricular or community activities, culture, socio-economic status, sex, race, ethnicity, religion, or sexual orientation would contribute to the diversity of the entering class and hence to your classmates' law school experience, you may describe these factors and their relevance in a separate diversity statement.*

We believe that you should not consider this diversity essay/statement "optional" at all, however, and recommend that you plan to submit one when offered the opportunity. You should take advantage of this invitation to present an aspect of yourself that will set you apart from other applicants and convince the admissions committee that you would be a welcome addition to the next class. This essay is an opportunity to convey a vibrant, sincere impression of your personality to the admissions reader. Note that a diversity essay is usually shorter than a personal statement would be. We recommend limiting yourself to approximately one double-spaced page, though typically, schools do not stipulate an exact length guideline for this essay.

Many law school applicants who do not belong to a readily recognizable minority group will question whether they can truly write an effective diversity statement. However, diversity in this context encompasses much more than the usual parameters of race, ethnicity, and sexual orientation. Any aspect of your character or past that could be classified as unique in some way—perhaps you spent time volunteering in the developing world, or diligently overcame an obstacle that facilitated a unique perspective, or possess a special talent that one does not encounter every day—can be compelling fodder for this kind of essay. Simply put, you do not have to write about standing out as a minority (though you can, if this applies to you), you just need to be thoughtful about your experiences and share them in a way that informs the reader that you have perspective and something special to contribute.

Showing rather than telling—which we explain in more detail later in this chapter—is of utmost importance in this essay, and is demonstrated in the following sample, in which the author writes about overcoming her struggle with attention deficit hyperactivity disorder.

SAMPLE OPTIONAL DIVERSITY ESSAY

"Every good boy deserves fudge" and "All cows eat grass." They may strike you as nonsensical statements, but these mnemonic devices added much-needed sense and sensibility to my life when I was young, helping guide my unsure fingers to the proper keys on our family's centuries-old piano. They served as beacons of focus in my quickly spinning mind, after I was diagnosed with attention deficit hyperactivity disorder (ADHD). My mother, convinced that music would be my saving grace, would quietly watch my progress, anxiously wringing her hands.

I approached each new piece of music with an arsenal of markers and highlighters, marking each section with a different color so I could more easily identify the important transitions and changes. Soon the pages of music would be covered in shades of pink, blue, purple, green, and yellow. Then, after I had spent many hours working on phrasing, rubato, and dynamics, my fingers would finally glide across the piano keys without interruption, as though I were performing in front of thousands of admiring fans at Carnegie Hall. In school, my peers would heckle me whenever I struggled to respond to a surprise question from the teacher—so often, my mind would wander and I would lose my place in my studies—and my self-confidence would falter, but at home, I pounded on the piano as confidently as Lang Lang strutting his stuff as "the J-Lo of the piano." Playing allowed me to finally exhale, as the beauty and emotion of the music overtook me and I became one with the piano. Following the various colors across the pages as the sections of notes melded into one cohesive melody helped me learn to really focus and gave me invaluable practice in following things through to the end.

As an adult, I feel I have mostly outgrown my ADHD. Sometimes, though, when I can feel myself growing irritable and my concentration starts to wane, I head straight for my piano. As I practice arpeggios and Beethoven's ten sonatas, a wave of calm and cheerfulness engulfs me, my mind clears, and my breathing becomes relaxed and regular again. I know then that I am able to tackle any work I have in front of me. Whenever I need it, I have an arsenal—and a rainbow—of brilliant compositions at hand.

This essay is effective because in highlighting one of the candidate's unique characteristics, it simultaneously demonstrates that she possesses confidence, willpower, and drive, in addition to a proven strategy for dealing with stress, which will no doubt serve her well in law school. She thereby impresses upon the admissions committee that she has the skills necessary to successfully deal with the challenges of earning a JD without ever having to state this directly.

§ PREPARING OUTLINES FOR YOUR ESSAYS

Years of experience have proven to us at jdMission that virtually all law school applicants are better off creating outlines for their essays before beginning to write the first full drafts. You are a busy person, so why not bring some efficiency and organization to the essay writing process?

Truth be told, many candidates' first reaction to the suggestion that they create outlines for their essays rather than simply diving into writing the first drafts is not a positive one. They imagine that this "extra" step will add unnecessary time and complication, when in fact, creating outlines can both facilitate the essay writing process and improve the final product. By taking the time to first organize your thoughts in the form of shorter phrases and terms, you will more easily see how your story unfolds and ensure that no gaps occur in the information you are trying to convey. This means a stronger, more persuasive final essay and, in most cases, fewer rounds of editing and revision, which saves time.

THE OUTLINE AS ROADMAP

Think of your essay outline as a kind of roadmap, one that guides you smoothly from the beginning of your story to the end, noting each important milestone along the way. Each major heading—or, if you prefer, each bullet point—should therefore consist of a very brief summary of a bigger idea. In other words, it should capture your key point but should not include the background, explanation, or descriptive details, leaving those for the full text of the essay. Simply put, your outline is meant to provide a concise overview of what you intend to write in your actual essay.

When constructing your outline, you can use very informal language, and you do not need to use full sentences or even proper grammar. After all, you are not submitting your outline to anyone—it is for "internal use only," so to speak.

Again, keep in mind that your outline should be just a brief overview of your longer essay. In general, we recommend that your outline be no longer than approximately 50% of the total word or page count allowed for the final essay. For example, using eight bullet points of 100 words each to outline what will be a 500-word essay would be pointless—your outline would be longer than your final essay, and this would not facilitate a more organized, efficient, or enjoyable writing experience.

THE SUPER SUMMARY

Your first step in outlining any essay is to compose one very clear sentence that captures the key idea that ties your entire essay together. This "super summary" of your essay will help you focus your thoughts and structure your work, much like a thesis sentence would for a more scientific or theoretical text. This is a nuanced but important point: for your law school application essays, you are not attempting to use a thesis to "prove" a point factually but instead are trying to construct a narrative that describes a central idea or experience from your life. So, you may start out with a well-structured outline and a clear thesis, but these will likely be softened and made less explicit in your first and subsequent drafts.

In Sample Essay A, which appears in full later in this section, the candidate is answering the following question posed by a top school: "Think about what you would want to convey in an interview and what you would bring to the law school. This may include your background, unique experiences, and the things that interest and motivate you." As you will see, the applicant has chosen to write about her decision to transition from her established career as a Wall Street investment banker to become a lawyer. A good super summary for her to build her essay around might then be: *Although I had established a successful and satisfying career in finance, a comment my grandfather made about the role of lawyers in business caused me to reevaluate what I want from my profession and decide to pursue a JD.*

This super summary works well because it presents the structure of the entire essay in one concise sentence. You now know exactly what the essay is going to discuss and how the essay will be focused. From this sentence, the candidate could then organize a structure for the essay, creating a loose outline of its key paragraphs, as follows:

Super Summary: *"Although I had established a successful and satisfying career in finance, a comment my grandfather made about the role of lawyers in business caused me to reevaluate what I want from my profession and decide to pursue a JD."*

Paragraph 1: Explanation of candidate's original career interest and choices

Paragraph 2: Development of skills in finance and establishment of Wall Street career

Paragraph 3: Introduction of new view of lawyers

Paragraph 4: Personal experience with lawyers on Wall Street

Paragraph 5: Solidification of candidate's desire to become a lawyer

BREAKING IT DOWN

Now, to create a logical and defined structure for these paragraphs, some short bullet points should be added that support the central idea within each one. Once this has been done, writing the actual essay becomes much less difficult. Consider the following:

Paragraph 1: Explanation of candidate's original career interest and choices

- Did not have aspirations to become a lawyer, despite family's involvement in the legal field

- Found business angle of parents' careers more appealing than the legal elements

Paragraph 2: Development of skills in finance and establishment of Wall Street career

- Earned BS with finance concentration

- Interned with Citigroup and then joined the company after graduation

Paragraph 3: Introduction of new view of lawyers

- Read exciting story of hostile business takeover

- Discussed book with grandfather, who made an illuminating comment about the role of lawyers in business

- Spent hours reevaluating her perception of the lawyers in the transaction described in the book

Paragraph 4: Personal experience with lawyers on Wall Street

- Saw anger and chaos ensue when a possible deal was jeopardized

- Witnessed lawyers working together calmly amid turmoil and ultimately facilitating a successful resolution of the issue

Paragraph 5: Solidification of candidate's desire to become a lawyer

- Developed interest in a JD and discussed this with family members

- Worked increasingly with lawyers on Wall Street and enjoyed the interactions and collaboration

- Has recognized the appropriateness of a career in law and is eager to get started

Again, we wish to stress that your outline is meant to serve as a guide for writing your narrative, but should not dictate your essay's definitive and inalterable final structure. If, while composing your essay, you think of a new takeaway you had overlooked when drafting your outline, or you feel that the essay is taking shape in a slightly different way, that is fine—you would simply need to revise your outline accordingly, ensuring that the amended version still works as a roadmap, effectively guiding the reader from the beginning of your story to the end, and that all the key milestones along the way make sense within context. The overarching idea here is to use the outline to organize your thoughts and to start yourself in the right direction with a clear foundation.

And here is the actual essay, following the sample outline.

Sample Essay A

"Think about what you would want to convey in an interview and what you can contribute to the law school. This may include your background, unique experiences, and the things that interest and motivate you." (2–3 pages)

Despite my family background—my father chairs the bankruptcy practice at a top Washington, DC, firm and my mother is a staff lawyer at the Securities and Exchange Commission—I did not grow up with the intention of attending law school. Although our family conversations often centered on law-related subjects, the underlying commercial business concerns that drove my parents' work are what captivated me, not the legalities. I therefore focused my education in a different direction.

After completing high school, I earned a BS with a concentration in finance from the University of Pennsylvania's Wharton undergraduate program, where I excelled academically and was president of Wharton Women my senior year. My two most significant summer internships were both with Citigroup, first in Manhattan and later in Buenos Aries, where I deepened my finance knowledge while improving my already-strong Spanish language skills. When I graduated in 2009 amidst a grim job market, I was able to land a global banking analyst position in Citigroup's New York office.

The summer before I began at Citigroup, I gathered with my family for the Fourth of July weekend at my grandparents' cottage in Minnesota. With my Wall Street position not commencing until after Labor Day, I decided to remain at the cottage with my grandparents after the rest of my family had gone home, and planned to spend my days reading on their dock. One day, I picked up Barbarians at the Gate: The Fall of RJR Nabisco, *the famous thriller about the company's hostile takeover in 1988, and found myself immediately engrossed in the story.*

When I finished the book a few days later, my grandfather, who is a retired judge, asked me what I had thought of it—and especially of the lawyers in the story. Having read the story with my usual focus on the finance side of things, I replied that I had noted only that the lawyers were present in their "traditional supporting role." We chatted about the book a little longer, and then, just as he was turning in for the night, my grandfather made a comment that changed how I viewed my new job—and even my intended career. He explained that most people see lawyers as technocrats who simply create a paper trail for their clients' transactions, but then added, "In fact, a lawyer's real job is to bring wisdom to the turmoil." I lay in bed that night for several hours, mulling over the book from a completely new angle and totally reevaluating my original assessment of the lawyers' role in the events it described. Although my grandfather and I did not revisit our conversation again before I left to begin my job at the end of the summer, I never really stopped thinking about it, and I returned to Citigroup with some new perspectives stirring in the back of my mind.

Six months later, I was part of a group of overworked bankers, auditors, and lawyers who were still up at 3:00 a.m., frantically scrambling to close a major deal, when suddenly we hit a serious snag. Almost immediately, tem-

pers began to flare. A significant piece of the deal hung in the balance, and the underlying reason for the transaction was severely undermined. Surveying the angry, chaotic scene, I noticed that the lawyers from both sides had separated themselves from the fray and gathered in the corner, speaking purposefully yet calmly. A few minutes later, the lead partner announced that the lawyers might have identified a solution. "Everyone go home and get some sleep," he said. "We'll have something for you by 10 tomorrow morning." And they did. As a result, we were able to make just a modest adjustment to the deal and close as originally scheduled. My grandfather's words again rang in my head: when everyone else had become overwhelmed and lost focus, the lawyers had managed to "bring wisdom to the turmoil."

Since then, I have become more and more interested in earning a JD. I have had extensive conversations on the topic with my parents and my grandfather, and I have found myself working more closely with the lawyers on my transactions than with any of the other bankers—and thoroughly enjoying it. More than once, lawyers have told me that they have never met an investment banker as interested in the law as I am. After three years on Wall Street, I have truly enjoyed my career in finance, but I now recognize that I want more. In the short term, I want to join with others who share my enthusiasm for the law in pursuit of a JD and bring my collaborative nature and background in finance to the law school community. In the long term, I want my work to be imbued with wisdom, and this fuels my desire to earn a law degree. I may not have started out wanting to be a lawyer, but I have come to realize that this career path is indeed the right one for me, and I am eager to make the transition.

§ WRITING EFFECTIVE ESSAYS

Writing your law school essays may be an entirely new writing experience for you. Perhaps you wrote some history essays or English literature papers in college, or maybe this is the first time you have needed to write since high school. If you *do* have some experience writing formal essays, we suspect you are most likely used to proving an argument in your text, not communicating an image of yourself through an introspective personal essay. In this section, we will present some tactics you can use to better convey your personality and unique qualities in your essays and to grab and keep your admissions reader's attention.

USING A NARRATIVE APPROACH

A traditional essay is generally one in which the writer presents information in an analytic and straightforward way in an attempt to prove a point. A narrative, on the other hand, involves the telling of a story; the writer essentially uses words to paint a kind of verbal picture of an event. Narratives are categorized by a comparatively subtle approach to writing, wherein the central facts of the story being conveyed are not just bluntly introduced but are presented in a way that lets them speak for themselves and paint a rounded picture of an experience. In your law school application essays, you are expected to talk about yourself—essentially, to tell your story to the admissions committee—rather than to argue a point, so a narrative approach is particularly fitting in this context. Note that all of the sample essays we present in this chapter take this kind of an approach. Essays written in a narrative, or "storytelling," style tend to be more compelling and interesting to read, and would therefore be more likely to grab and maintain an admissions reader's attention.

Consider the following two essay introductions:

Example A: *Soccer is a national passion and way of life in Colombia. As a Colombian myself, I have been playing soccer constantly since I could walk, when I laced up my cleats for the first time. I shared my passion for soccer with the children of Colombian immigrants in the United States, helping them reconnect with their heritage and building their confidence. This challenging and rewarding experience is one that I am far better for having participated in.*

Example B: *"GOOOOOOOL! GOL! GOL! GOL!" Every day for two years, at exactly 4:00 a.m., my father would wake me with this unique alarm, so that I would be on time for my morning soccer drills with America de Cali, a professional soccer team in Colombia with whom I had the privilege of training when I was young. Although my dreams of playing professionally ended after I later suffered a serious knee injury, I continued to play for the joy of the game, the companionship and the pride it brought, and I was fortunate to share these benefits with the teenage children of Colombian immigrants I met when I first arrived in the United States.*

Which of these openings resonates more with you and creates a more compelling image of the writer? We expect that you would choose Example B! Example A follows more of a traditional approach, involving a declarative, thesis-like statement that explicitly tells the reader the central point of the essay. Example B uses a narrative approach, engaging the reader in a story that will ultimately—but much more subtly—convey the very same points as it unfolds.

First-Person Perspective

A narrative relies much more heavily on the **first-person perspective**. Consider the line "soccer is a national passion and a way of life in Colombia" from Example A. This is a statement of fact that focuses on things other than the writer, not a first-person description of a personal experience like we see in Example B.

Sense of Ownership

Complementing this first-person perspective is a **sense of ownership**. "Soccer is a national passion and a way of life" is not a statement that applies exclusively to the writer. In fact, this objective statement could be made by just about anyone (such generic statements are especially to be avoided in application essays). In contrast, that many people would share the exact same experience of wanting to give their immigrant cousins a different perspective on life by teaching them soccer is rather improbable—which means the chances of two people both writing the sentences used in Example B are almost nil. By creating truly personal statements based on your unique experiences, you alone own the story, and this can help set you apart from the competition when you are applying to law school.

Simplicity

One concern many applicants have is that a narrative approach might be difficult to execute, but we firmly believe that writing in a narrative style is actually easier than writing a traditional essay, because the writer needs only to consider and then convey the events and experiences as they actually occurred. Writing a narrative does not require using long, complex sentences or sophisticated adjectives with multiple syllables. In fact, **simplicity** is truly the rule. Once again, consider Example B. The language is not particularly elaborate— "companionship" may be the most complex word used!

Momentum

To construct an effective narrative, you want to be sure to maintain the **momentum** in your story—that your description of the experience is constantly moving forward. To do this, continuously ask yourself, "And then what happened?," and generally, you should be able to keep reporting the events as they occurred. As long as your core story is strong and you maintain a connection from sentence to sentence, writing the details of your narrative should allow you to create an interesting essay. After all, you are simply relating a personal experience you had, not trying to prove a thesis or make disconnected facts fit together in a comprehensive way. When you start your essay with an overarching and generic statement such as "Soccer is a national passion and way of life in Colombia," knowing how to answer the question "And then what happened?" and getting the story to unfold from there is much more difficult. In a successful narrative essay, each sentence serves as a crucial link in the story, so one way to test whether this has been achieved is to remove a sentence from the essay, read the piece again, and see if the story still makes sense.

Earnestness

In addition, writing an essay using a narrative approach facilitates a certain earnestness. In Example A, the writer states, "As a Colombian myself, I have been playing soccer constantly since I could walk." Although this is not as blunt as telling the reader straight out, "I am a great soccer player," it still uses stark language. In Example B, however, the reader learns that the individual is passionate about soccer but does so by witnessing the writer's passion rather than simply being told it exists. The reader naturally understands it from the nature and tone of the narrative.

§ SHOWING VERSUS TELLING

Perhaps you have heard the journalistic maxim "Show, don't tell!" Indeed, this maxim is an important one to keep in mind when drafting your application essays, and it definitely captures the essence of narrative writing. Rather than *telling* your reader that you are passionate about something, *show* your reader by relating a personal experience. Consider the following examples of telling versus showing:

Example A:

> **Tell**: *I have always been interested in the safety and welfare of children, and I will go to extreme lengths to help a child.*

Show: When I saw a child being taunted at the local school bus stop, I quickly parked and offered to walk the boy to school, even though I was already late for work.

Example B:

Tell: I love to travel and have visited more than 20 countries on four continents, primarily in the Middle East, where I became fluent in various Arabic dialects.

Show: Algeria, Tunisia, Morocco, and Egypt—after six months in these countries, I found myself comfortably speaking colloquial Arabic over tea with the locals.

Again, you will notice that although the underlying message is the same in each set of examples, the method of conveying the message is quite different. When you *show* an idea or experience in your writing, you invite your reader into your story and have a better chance of maintaining that person's attention from that point on.

Consider again our sample diversity essay by the candidate with ADHD. Rather than simply stating that she used her piano practice to learn to deal with and overcome the symptoms of her disorder, she recounts the process and events as they unfolded, thereby conjuring a series of images that leads the reader to the conclusions she wants to convey. Likewise, she imparts certain emotions through descriptions rather than direct adjectives. For example, she communicates her mother's nervousness not by simply declaring that her mother worried that practicing the piano might not be beneficial, but by describing how her mother "would quietly watch…, anxiously wringing her hands." The candidate does not simply present a series of facts and then inform the reader how he or she should feel about those facts, but instead lets the story make the desired impression.

§ Necessary Conflict

Every effective story must involve a clear conflict. By this, we mean conflict in the literary sense, not in the physical or emotional sense (no one wants to hear about a candidate who hotheadedly instigates repeated confrontations). In literary terms, conflict occurs when an oppositional force helps shape the course of a story. So, a story in which you are the hero and are enjoying a very smooth ride toward victory will not be as interesting or exciting as a story in which you encountered an obstacle or two along the way.

For example, most people would find the story of a rookie runner beating an experienced marathoner at the finish line significantly more compelling than the story of an experienced marathoner beating all his or her fellow runners by a wide margin, never experiencing any real competition. The former scenario involves a conflict in the form of an unexpected upset (the experienced marathoner losing to a rookie), whereas the latter presents a situation with no inherent surprise or suspense. So, as you work to identify the stories you will showcase in your application essays, consider the hurdles you have overcome in your life, because those narratives are the ones that will allow you to shine more brightly.

With this new perspective in mind, let us revisit the sample essays we presented earlier in this chapter. In our sample traditional personal statement, the candidate is shocked to learn that her cultural heritage—which, because of her grandfather, is such an important part of who she is—is little understood or considered by her current country's government and citizens, and she develops a desire to see a change both among and for her fellow Indian Americans. In our sample free-form essay, the candidate identified something missing in the lives of a group of teenagers and used his skills as a soccer coach to help the teenagers become more cohesive, connect better with their immigrant parents, and develop a sense of pride. In our sample diversity essay, the central conflict is introduced within the first few sentences when the candidate with ADHD alludes to the complications her disorder causes, and begins describing her unique approach to overcoming them.

If the writers of these essays had not taken the initiative to respond to their situations, they would have no story to tell. Their reactions to the conflicts they encountered and the changes they subsequently effected are what shape their stories and make them interesting. Each of the stories you use in your essays should therefore involve a clear conflict—an oppositional force of some kind—to hold the reader's attention and maintain the narrative's momentum.

§ Required Structural Elements

Well-written narratives include five important structural elements: an introduction/exposition, rising action, a climax, falling action, and a conclusion/dénouement. The **introduction/exposition** provides the context for the story, allowing the reader to understand the characters and the setting in which the conflict exists. Then, the **rising action** describes the steps taken and the obstacles encountered by the writer as he or she strives to resolve the story's central conflict. Next comes the **climax**, which is a moment of change, a turning point that determines whether the writer will ultimately succeed or fail. Subsequently, during the **falling action**, the action winds down, and the results of the writer's actions are described. And finally, during the **conclusion/dénouement**, the story is brought to a close, with the writer's ambitions either satisfied or unsatisfied. Sometimes, the author may also reflect briefly on the outcome.

To illustrate, let us identify these structural elements as they appear in the sample free-form essay by the youth soccer coach:

"GOOOOOOOL! GOL! GOL! GOL!" Every day for two years, at exactly 4:00 a.m., my father would wake me with this unique alarm, so that I would be on time for my morning soccer drills with America de Cali, a professional soccer team in Colombia with whom I had the privilege of training when I was young. Although my dreams of playing professionally

ended after I later suffered a serious knee injury, I continued to play for the joy of the game, the companionship and the pride it brought, and I was fortunate to share these benefits with the teenage children of Colombian immigrants I met when I first arrived in the United States.

Growing up, my friends and I imagined the United States as a place where anything and everything fortuitous could happen to us immediately upon arrival. When, at the age of 25, I first visited my aunts and their families in Union City, New Jersey, however, very little in their lives resembled the images from my youthful imagination youthful imagination of what life in America was supposed to be like. Instead of the big, beautiful houses we had conjured in our dreams, their "houses" were actually just single rooms, each one occupied by a large family, with all the families sharing cramped amenities. My relatives worked long hours just to pay the bills, and my cousins rarely left their apartments, let alone Union City. I understood struggle, having experienced it firsthand, but I could not accept the despondency and defeat I saw in the eyes of my aunts, their family members, and their neighbors. I wanted to give my cousins and their friends, who were also the children of immigrants, a window into a different world, and I did so using—of all things—a mere soccer ball. A quick pick-up game with my cousins slowly turned into weekly lessons/practices with them and a group of their peers, and they would regularly play late into the night. With America de Cali, I had learned how to run clinics that were practical yet fun, and I was able to use these skills to coach my cousins and their friends. In time, I began to see a new light in these young people's eyes. [The first two paragraphs of this essay serve as the **introduction/exposition** and gradually introduce the central conflict, as the writer comes to realize the deficiencies in the teenagers' lives.]

The teenagers I found myself coaching had grown up immersed in U.S. culture—they were fans of American football and rooted for the New York Giants, they barely spoke their native Spanish, and for them, soccer was but a newborn pastime in the United States. Their interests and experience in

America thus far had created a separation between them and their parents, who did not share the teenagers' appreciation for American football and lamented the loss of a connection with their children that the language barrier had caused. However, as they watched their children learn and develop a passion for the sport of their youth, this gap began to close. My insistence that we all speak only Spanish during practice aided this process. We also "adopted" a soccer team from Pereira, Colombia—my hometown—and followed its games enthusiastically throughout the season. [Here in the **rising action**, we see the obstacles that complicate the central conflict and the steps the writer takes to help the teenagers.] *As a result, the kids gained a sense of belonging to something larger than their isolated immigrant community in Union City. Once this initial connection was established, I was able to also teach them about Pereira's remarkable coffee culture, about Colombia's distinguished heritage, and about their own great cultural inheritance. I now saw pride in their faces—pride in themselves and in their community.* [Here in the **climax**, the writer describes the way his creative approaches created change for the teenagers.]

As the soccer season drew to a close, our weekly games were soon replaced by fiestas each weekend at a different player's home, and everyone was invited. To the sounds of vallenatos *(traditional music of Colombia), we ate* arepa de choclo *(corn cakes), sopa de sancocho (chicken stew), and, our favorite,* chocolate con pan *(bread soaked in homemade chocolate). During these parties, the older teenagers, many of whom were ready for their first full-time job, would talk about their aspirations for the future. These conversations sometimes led to informal internships with my friends and acquaintances in New York City that I helped arrange. For example, one of the players went to work for a friend of mine from Brazil who had just started an event planning company in midtown Manhattan. Another came to work for my wife in her family's restaurant so he could learn about restaurant management. These young people's eyes were opened to the wonderfully vibrant city in their backyard as well as to the innumerable and exciting opportunities it offered.* [In the **falling action**, the writer presents the subsequent effects on the teenagers of the resolution of the central conflict. The reader sees the results of the writer's actions.]

These kids' fervor for soccer led them to embrace their hyphenated identities, to be proud U.S. citizens of Latin American descent. This in turn gave them the confidence to strive for more in their lives in this country and set the stage for future success. As any soccer player will attest, true magic can be found in the spin of a soccer ball. [In the **conclusion**, the writer explains that he was successful in his efforts to help the teenagers, and reflects on the experience.]

§ A Special Focus on Introductions

Applicants tend to struggle most with their law school essays at the very beginning of the writing process. Even when you have a strong outline in hand, crafting those first few words or phrases can often be challenging. In this section, we focus on composing strong introductions in hopes of helping you more easily overcome this hurdle when you begin drafting your application essays.

A Powerful Opening Line

"It is a truth universally acknowledged, that a single man in possession of a good fortune, must be in want of a wife."

"Happy families are all alike; every unhappy family is unhappy in its own way."

"It was a bright, cold day in April, and the clocks were striking thirteen."

Some who read these lines may recognize them from the novels from which they came: Jane Austen's *Pride and Prejudice*, Leo Tolstoy's *Anna Karenina,* and George Orwell's *1984*, respectively. However, fewer will have actually read these works, and some may be largely unfamiliar with them and their authors—yet they may still recognize these opening lines. Our point? A powerful first line can stick with people long after they have finished reading a story, and sometimes even when they have not read the story at all!

MAINTAINING THE MYSTERY

Although you do not need to write with the flair and drama of an internationally acclaimed author, you *do* need to carefully consider your essay's opening statement and ensure that you are capturing your reader's imagination.

Consider two of the introductory sentences we have offered thus far in this chapter:

> *"GOOOOOOOL! GOL! GOL! GOL!" Every day for two years, at exactly 4:00 a.m., my father would wake me with this unique alarm, so that I would be on time for my morning soccer drills with America de Cali, a professional soccer team in Colombia with whom I had the privilege of training when I was young.*

> *"Good boys deserve fudge always" and "All cows eat grass."*

These openers are designed to "tease" and naturally compel the reader to want to continue reading. Many prospective JDs give far too much away in the opening sentences of their application essays and present the solution to their story's central conflict right away (through a "tell"), which only succeeds in losing the reader's attention immediately. (Remember, if you lose your admissions reader in this way, you risk losing your admissions *offer*, too.)

Consider the following examples of opening lines that present no mystery at all:

By coaching soccer, I showed a group of teenagers a life outside their immediate confines, both literally and figuratively.

As a child, I was diagnosed with attention deficit hyperactivity disorder and used playing piano as a means of overcoming the challenges I faced as a result.

If you begin your law school application essay with this kind of opener, where do you go next? What can the reader really learn about you or the story you want to tell after one of these introductory sentences? Very little, unfortunately, and giving away the crux of your narrative in the first sentence makes writing the rest of your essay much more difficult. So, keep in mind that a narrative starts with a "blast" and then slowly unfolds—the most interesting point of your essay should never be revealed in the very first sentence.

HISTORICAL VERSUS ANECDOTAL OPENING

Some law school candidates choose to take a straightforward, historical approach to their stories in their essays. Nothing is fundamentally wrong with this tactic, and it can be an easy way to organize an essay. However, when taking a historical approach, the writer may miss the opportunity to offer a more focused and gripping introduction, beginning the essay by presenting straightforward chronological facts rather than something more compelling. Under certain circumstances, an anecdotal opening can better grab the reader's interest. Consider the following example of a historical opening:

To the shock of my friends and family, I eschewed an offer from a major investment bank after graduating from college and instead chose an unpaid internship with the nonprofit organization Engineers in Africa. I was on the front lines of the battle to bring clean water to Liberian communities, literally digging wells with locals, taking my turn with the shovel for hours. Over time, our hand tools and our manmade drills led to buckets and pools of water and then to a basic pipeline from the well to the town center. Forty families soon drank truly fresh water for the first time in their village's history.

This introduction is very direct and informative—and entirely acceptable—but the writer might more successfully capture the reader's attention if he or she were to use an anecdotal opening instead, as shown in the following example:

Although my back was killing me, I could not let my Liberian hosts know. As I took my turn with the shovel, I prayed to see water abruptly spring forth under its blade. We had been working for two straight days and had even created a rudimentary drill, trying to bring life to a freshwater well that I had sited, which we hoped would bring fresh drinking water to the 40 families in the area—and to my own cup, as well. Suddenly, I noticed that the ground was wet. I alerted the rest of the team, and we started to dig faster and with renewed enthusiasm. Before nightfall, we were reeling up bucket after bucket of cool, clear water. Before the end of the week, we had constructed a simple pipeline that carried the water into the town center. I was 12 weeks into my career and could not have felt more confident that I had made the right choice in declining a position with a major investment bank and flying to Liberia with Engineers in Africa instead.

In this second, anecdotal version, much of the same basic information is conveyed, but the visual appeal is much stronger—the author paints a more colorful, complete, and engaging picture. We believe that after having read hundreds, if not thousands, of other application essays, an admissions reader would respond much more readily to a compelling introduction such as this. That said, however, one style of opening is not necessarily right and the other is not wrong. What matters is that you are comfortable with whichever approach you choose. So take time to consider which one is a better fit with the narrative you intend to present. Depending on your story, an anecdotal opening may more easily allow you to capture your reader's imagination.

Non-Introduction Introduction

Because candidates often feel that they have to explicitly present the point they intend to make in their essay in their opening lines, many end up crafting long and often uninteresting introductions that do not actually convey anything important (and use up valuable word count/page space). In the case of law school admissions essays, you are typically better served by simply launching into the action of your story and expecting that the reader will remain interested throughout the remainder of the narrative.

Once again, consider these two sample introductions:

> *"GOOOOOOOL! GOL! GOL! GOL!" Every day for two years, at exactly 4:00 a.m., my father would wake me with this unique alarm, so that I would be on time for my morning soccer drills with America de Cali, a professional soccer team in Colombia with whom I had the privilege of training when I was young.*

> *"Good boys deserve fudge always" and "All cows eat grass."*

Neither of these examples includes a long "windup" to set the stage for the coming action. Instead, the writer launches directly into the story he or she wants to tell. This approach both engages the reader in the story right away and minimizes word use, so more space is available to include more important details of the candidate's narrative.

§ Word Count and Maximum Page Count

In general, sticking as closely to requested word and page limits as possible is a good idea. Doing so indicates to the admissions committee not only that you pay attention to and can follow directions (which reflects positively on you as a potential student who will be required to follow numerous guidelines throughout the course of the JD program) but also that you are willing to put in the work required to convey your story effectively within the stated parameters. Also, you show respect for both the school and the admissions committee members, who must sort through thousands of essays each week. Note that some schools specify a maximum page count instead of a word count. In such cases, pay close attention to requested font size, margin size, and spacing, and contact the school's admissions office for clarification, if necessary. Still other schools allow candidates to decide for themselves the length of their essay. Making such a call can be challenging, but we recommend targeting a total word count that is comparable to what the other schools to which you are applying stipulate.

CHAPTER 3

PREPARING A STANDOUT RÉSUMÉ

Imagine that you are trying to find your way around a major city with which you are somewhat—or perhaps even totally—unfamiliar. Let us use New York City as an example. Suddenly, to your relief, someone hands you a map the size of a standard sheet of paper (8½" × 11"), only it has every single street, park, school, city, government building, business, and landmark in the area labeled on it. Most likely, this map would be more overwhelming and perplexing than helpful. Rather than a tool that clearly delineates the most important information you need to get where you want to go, you would have a chaotic assortment of too much information, creating more confusion than clarity.

Now imagine instead that someone hands you a map of the city, but only the major thoroughfares and landmarks are shown. You can clearly distinguish the principal avenues and cross streets and a few significant buildings and spaces, such as Central Park, the headquarters of the United Nations, Rockefeller Center, and the Empire State Building. If you were a first-time visitor to New York and trying to quickly orient yourself to the city, which map would you want to use? Our guess is that you would choose the second, more sparse—and therefore more practical—map. Although it might not be helpful in leading you into every nook and cranny in the city (though, we must note, neither would the first map), it would certainly provide the basic information necessary to understand New York's layout and to help you navigate your way to your intended destination.

To an outsider, your résumé is a kind of "map" to who you are, and have been, professionally. This document quickly familiarizes the reader with your career's major highlights (the landmarks) and your unique skills and accomplishments (the streets and tourist attractions). Unfortunately, when writing a résumé—whether for law school, a job application, or any other reason—most people try to include every single bit of information about themselves and end up with a résumé that is nearly impossible to use, like the first map we described. However, a résumé that instead focuses solely on the most significant data points about the individual—like the second map we described—allows readers to quickly identify and comprehend the writer's major achievements and his or her academic, professional, and even life story.

As you approach your résumé, really think about what you want the individual reading your résumé to *absorb*, rather than what you are worried he or she might miss. You will find yourself in a far better position if someone takes the time to read 100% of the information you provide, even if it represents only 50% of the potential content you could glean from your life, rather than 0% of the information, because you have overloaded your résumé with every possible detail. Try putting yourself in the shoes of an admissions officer who has to sort through thousands of files; admissions officers have neither the time nor the desire to have to hunt for the relevant information in your résumé. Instead, they want you to make their lives easier and their jobs more efficient. They want you to provide that simple map, with all the important landmarks!

And we cannot stress this enough: please (we beg of you!) do not just hand in whatever you have been compiling since you first applied for a job in the tenth grade. Your résumé is not a throwaway, but an important element of your law school application and a valuable opportunity to make a statement about yourself to the admissions committee!

As you strive to make your statement, keep in mind that the two most important aspects of constructing your résumé are properly managing your space and crafting compelling bullets. If you can nail these two components, you should be much of the way toward drafting a résumé that the admissions committee can really use. And is that not the point?

§ Creating Your New Résumé

From here on out, we are going to take a top down approach to creating your new résumé (your career map) and we mean that literally. We are going to start with a blank page and construct a résumé from scratch, offering "dos and don'ts" along the way.

LENGTH AND FORMATTING

Before you even put your fingers on your keyboard, you should take a step back and get into the mind-set that you are creating a one-page résumé. We have already discussed how "less is more"—which is why we advise virtually every law school candidate to submit one-page résumés—it is an easier map to comprehend. Some schools may allow you to submit a two-page résumé, but in such cases, do not feel that you *must* use all of the space available. Harvard Law School actually posts three sample résumés on its website that the admissions committee feels are effective.[5] Of the three, two are only one page long, and the third is not quite one and a half pages long, supporting our point that your résumé does not have to be extensive to be effective, and in fact may be more powerful by being more concise. If you choose to submit a two-page résumé (and please do not submit anything longer!), your reader may have difficulty scanning, identifying, and remembering your important facts.

You might suddenly be feeling a little bit squeezed for space. In order to make the most of that page, you do not need to reduce your margins to the nonexistently narrow or reduce the size of your font to the point where your reader needs a magnifying glass to see what you have written. Here are three space-saving tips that may allow you to discover "real estate" that you never knew you had:

1. *Do not* include a mission statement at the beginning of your résumé. Your mission in this case is quite clear—to gain admission to the law school program to which you are applying—and, of course, the admissions committee already knows this! A mission statement will take up precious space that can be used more effectively for other purposes.

---

5 Application Components, Harvard Law School Web page; accessed March 7, 2012, www. law.harvard.edu/prospective/jd/apply/the-application-process/resources.html.

2. Only your name should appear at the top of your résumé. You do not need to include your address, email address, gender, marital status, etc., because this information will all be provided in your application form. As with a mission statement, adding this kind of information will use up valuable space that you could instead use for other key points.

3. Your résumé should not state that you possess basic computer skills. Such proficiencies are expected today, and including them will take up space that could be better used for other, more unique information.

STRUCTURING YOUR CONTENT—SECTION BY SECTION

As you stare at that blank space, you need to determine how you will organize your content and that starts with determining which headings you will use to call out your important areas of competency. Education and Professional Experience are obviously standard, but what about Leadership/Activities, Publications/Research, Personal/Interests, and Awards—or even Military Experience and Entrepreneurial Experience? There are many ways for you to organize your résumé, but the point to keep in mind is that even though you have options, you should limit your headings to only those that are the most relevant and important to your life.

Headings serve to bring attention to the unique aspects of your résumé and establish a framework for a chronology that could otherwise be confusing. For example, if while you were working as a research assistant in college you simultaneously founded a start-up, the dates of these experiences will overlap. In such an instance, you would likely want to spate these experiences, including your research experience in your Education section or creating a separate Entrepreneurial Experience section in which to discuss your start-up. This would allow you to distinguish and highlight each of these accomplishments individually, rather than having them lumped together in one large Professional Experience section. Overlapping dates can easily slow a reader down!

In the résumé that we create in this chapter, assume that our prospective law student has a pretty standard set of experiences and his headings thus follow in a routine manner:

1. Education

2. Professional Experience

3. Extracurricular Activities

4. Personal

YOUR EDUCATION SECTION

Many law school candidates choose to start their résumés with a section about their academic experiences, because this aspect of their lives is more current and often more relevant to the admissions committee. This is almost always a good idea for a law school résumé, unless your professional experience has been quite significant and impressive. Of course, the adjectives "significant" and "impressive" are subjective, but if you feel that you have a few years of standout work experience, you may want to consider starting your résumé with an emphasis on this area.

Let us take a look at a sample Education section and see whether it adheres to the principles we have discussed thus far in this chapter:

Education

University of XYZ
Springfield, AK

Bachelor of Arts in Political Studies, GPA 3.7
2009

- Department Nominee, Faculty of Arts Undergraduate Student of the Year (2008)
- Smithson Language Study Scholarship (2008)
- *Daily XYZ'er*, Sports Editor (2007–2009)
- Teaching Assistant, International Political Economy (2008–2009)
- Co-Chair, Political Studies Student Conference (2007–2008)
- Dean's List, 2006, 2007, 2008, 2009

What can we observe about the Education entry? Is it a convenient, easy-to-read section of our map? The answer is... not at all! It is a hodgepodge of different accomplishments (activities and awards received are listed together), and the information is presented in a variety of dissimilar formats. Consider the first two bullet points. How do they differ? They actually have inconsistent structures, with the first offering a title of sorts (Department Nominee) to go along with the achievement (Faculty of Arts Undergraduate Student of the Year), whereas the second offers only the achievement (Smithson Language Study Scholarship). For consistency's sake, the bullets should instead read as follows:

- Department Nominee, Faculty of Arts Undergraduate Student of the Year (2008)

- Recipient, Smithson Language Study Scholarship (2008)

Another option would be the following:

- Faculty of Arts Undergraduate Student of the Year (2008)

- Smithson Language Study Scholarship (2008)

Ensuring consistency among your bullet points makes them easier to read and understand, and conveys a sense that you are an organized person who pays attention to details. Conversely, inconsistencies, especially when they begin to add up, can distract your reader. To maintain agreement with the style we have now introduced (we will continue with the first approach), the bullet about the candidate's experience as a "sports editor" should read as follows:

- Sports Editor, *Daily XYZ'er* (2007–2009)

However, this element of the writer's experience is an activity rather than an accomplishment or award, so if there were a variety of activities, listing them separately would impose more order on the résumé and render the information more noticeable and easier to grasp. We could therefore rewrite and reorganize the Education section as follows:

Education

University of XYZ   Springfield, AK
Bachelor of Arts in Political Studies, GPA 3.7   2009

Awards:

- Department Nominee, Faculty of Arts Undergraduate Student of the Year (2008)
- Recipient, Smithson Language Study Scholarship (2008)
- Recipient, Dean's List recognition (2006–2009)

Activities:

- Sports Editor, *Daily XYZ'er* (2007–2009)
- Teaching Assistant, International Political Economy (2008–2009)
- Co-Chair, Political Studies Student Conference (2007–2008)

Note that the discrepancy in the way the years were originally presented has also been adjusted for consistency: compare "2006, 2007, 2008, 2009" for the Dean's List item in the original example with "(2006–2009)" in this example.

YOUR ACTIVITIES SECTION

The sample in the previous section represents a perfectly acceptable way of arranging your Education section, but yet another option (and creating a résumé requires a lot of judgment) would be for this candidate to create separate Education and Activities sections altogether. (Again, not every candidate will use this section!) This would help facilitate readability by dividing the information into smaller, more delineated segments, but perhaps more importantly, this current format provides no real way of knowing whether this individual was effective as a sports editor, teaching assistant, or conference co-chair, because the candidate does not have enough room to elaborate on these activities without expanding the section even further.

So, to best flesh out this information, we can create a separate Activities section and add bullet points for each activity listed that reveal specific accomplishments. (We explain the importance of such bullets and offer tips on how to construct them later in this chapter.) Although less is more, we do not want to be so succinct that we do not provide the reader with enough information to appreciate notable experiences. Every decision is somewhat space dependent, but some applicants will have sufficient room for an Activities section, like the one that follows:

Activities

Daily XYZ'er   Springfield, AK
Sports Editor   2007–2009

- Managed a team of three sports journalists, ensuring accurate reporting and fulfillment of all deadline obligations
- Created "FANtastic sports minute" contest, generating 175 fan videos and 30,000 hits to *XYZ'er* website

Department of Political Studies   Springfield, AK
Teaching Assistant (TA), International Political Economy (IPE)   2008–2009

- Initiated a "week in review" study program that incorporated current events and academic review; program was subsequently adopted by two other IPE TAs

Political Studies Student Conference   Springfield, AK
Co-Chair (Nominated by Faculty and Student Committee)   2007–2008

- Raised $25,000 from corporate donors, ensuring the conference met all financial obligations
- Persuaded planning committee to open the conference to neighboring colleges, resulting in a 100% increase in attendance and a 35% increase in revenue

YOUR PROFESSIONAL EXPERIENCE SECTION

Now that our applicant's Education and Activities sections have been developed, let us move on and address his Professional Experience section, which follows:

Professional Experience

College Franchise Painter, Inc.   Springfield, AK
Franchisee   Summers 2008, 2009
- Acquired $10,000 in "friends and family" funding to purchase franchise; paid off loans and generated 11% return on investor capital in 2008
- Developed marketing campaign and relationships with contractors; generated $90,000 in revenue each summer
- Hired, trained, and maintained a staff of ten college painters throughout summer; typical franchise employee turnover is 20%
- Sold well-developed franchise to fellow student for $15,000, realizing a 50% return on initial franchise cost

Sports Stuff   Springfield, AK
Sales Specialist   2005–2008

- Maintained 20-hour workweek throughout the academic year, self-financing a significant portion of tuition and living expenses
- Developed snowboarding product knowledge and regularly hosted "teach-ins" for 12-member staff on product attributes

These entries are aesthetically identical to one another and to those in the Activities and Education sections we have already seen. What are some of the other consistencies we can note?

- Bolding of firm/organization's name

- Italicizing of position title

- Placement of locations and years

- Size of margins

You should note that the use of bold and italics plays a significant role in organizing your map. However, excessive use of these tools blunts their effect and dilutes their impact. Thus, reserve the use of emphasis tools to draw attention to such elements as your name, company names, and job titles. If everything is bold, nothing stands out!

As you examine the professional entries above, one point that deserves mention is that the longest entry in this faux résumé—College Franchise Painter—has only four bullet points. The more bullets you include, the less likely your reader will be to pay attention to all of them, so make sure to list only your most important and notable achievements. More than four or five will most likely overwhelm your reader and will dilute, if not completely nullify, the impression you are trying to make. (Remember: Less is more!)

We also suggest that if you have worked for a company you believe most people would not readily recognize or whose name does not clearly convey the type of business it is, you should include a simple one-line description of the firm *in italics*. Although many companies, and especially large and international ones, are known by most admissions committee readers, you cannot expect that everyone will be familiar with every organization mentioned in your résumé. Consider the following example, in which we have replaced Sports Stuff with Robertson's, which is a much more ambiguous name:

Robertson's   Springfield, AK
Sales Specialist   2005–2008
Robertson's is a three-location sporting goods megastore with 200 employees.
- Maintained 20-hour workweek throughout the academic year, self-financing a significant portion of tuition and living expenses
- Developed snowboarding product knowledge and regularly hosted "teach-ins" for 12-member staff on product attributes

YOUR PERSONAL SECTION

We strongly encourage you to include a brief Personal section at the end of your résumé in which you list your interests and hobbies, as appropriate. This kind of information helps to humanize you in the admissions committee's eyes and, in some cases, may even facilitate some sort of personal connection between you and the school representative who is reading your résumé—"You ran the New York City Marathon in 2011? I ran it in 2005!"

Be sure to be specific about your interests. For example, writing "Completed three Olympic-distance triathlons" is much more effective than writing simply "Triathlons" and also gives the reader more personalized information with which to evaluate you. Although you should always be careful to exercise restraint in this section, listing more unique interests such as steeplechasing or playing bagpipes (as long as you are truthful!) can really grab your reader's attention and make your résumé stand out.

The following is our sample candidate's personal section:

Personal
- Languages: Fluent in Spanish, conversational Arabic, conversational French
- Passions: Snowboarding, walking my dog (Phil) around Springfield, Chinese cooking (completed three classes)

The first line clearly outlines the candidate's proficiency in languages, which is valuable information for the reader, because it indicates the candidate's intellectual curiosity and capabilities. The second reveals his interests and, to some degree, even his personality. "Walking my dog (Phil) around Springfield" may not be an appropriate bullet point for everyone, but in this case, the candidate has included it to help reveal a sense of humor and to bring a little extra life and character to his résumé. And that is what this section is about—"life and character"—so don't "overshare," but also do not feel reluctant to offer insight into who you are beyond your traditional accomplishments.

Conveying Your Experience Through Bullet Points

We have discussed structure and consistency extensively, but what should you be writing about in each of your entries? Consider these sample bullet points from the examples we have already presented:

- Managed a team of three sports journalists, ensuring accurate reporting and fulfillment of all deadline obligations

- Developed marketing campaign and relationships with contractors; generated $90,000 in revenue each summer

- Maintained 20-hour workweek throughout the academic year, self-financing a significant portion of tuition and living expenses

- Persuaded planning committee to open the conference to neighboring colleges, resulting in a 100% increase in attendance and a 35% increase in revenue

We can make a few key observations about these bullets. First, they are all concise! None would be longer than two lines on a properly formatted résumé (note that this book is narrower than the typical 8½" × 11" page). Second, they all begin with action-oriented verbs: *managed, developed, maintained, persuaded* (we explain the importance of this later in this chapter). And finally, they all start with very deliberate actions and follow with very clear results.

ACTION VERBS

Each bullet point in a professional or extracurricular entry should begin with an action-oriented verb, such as *acquired, developed, hired, sold, raised,* or *persuaded.* These kinds of verbs, which indicate deliberate, focused action, make a strong impact on the reader. Conversely, take care to avoid words that may make your contributions seem vague or even ineffectual, as in the following examples:

- Helped team achieve target goals (*How did you help?*)

- Contributed to strategic planning meetings (*How did you contribute?*)

Words such as *helped* and *contributed* do not convey what you accomplished and thus do not promote you as someone who gets things done. (Consult the list of action-oriented verbs provided in Appendix D for assistance in choosing words that will bolster your résumé entries' effectiveness.) If you lead with action-oriented verbs and include clearly quantifiable results, you should have strong bullet points throughout your résumé.

Action/Results

Many individuals, when writing a résumé, inadvertently focus on describing their *responsibilities* in their bullet points, rather than their deliberate *actions* and consequent *results*. When only your responsibilities are presented—with no accompanying results—your reader has no way of knowing whether you were effective in the position you are describing. For example, consider the following entry, in which only the candidate's responsibilities are listed:

Political Studies Student Conference   Springfield, AK
Co-Chair (Nominated by Faculty and Student Committee)   2007–2008

- Managed all aspects of student conference, from corporate fundraising to tickets sales to arranging guest speakers
- Acted as a liaison between XYZ and other colleges in the surrounding area

After reading these bullet points, you might be left wondering, "Did this person *do a good job* of managing the conference?" This individual could easily have been the conference's best manager ever—or even its worst ever!—and you would have no idea one way or the other based on these bullets, because the only real information provided is minimal: he managed the conference. Maybe his fundraising efforts were insufficient. Or maybe they were so robust that the organization was able to start an endowment after the conference with the excess resources. We cannot possibly draw a conclusion either way using only the basic information presented.

Now consider the following rewrite of this entry, which focuses instead on the candidate's *effectiveness* in the position he held. These bullet points manage to reveal the candidate's level of competence by connecting specific actions with clear results.

Political Studies Student Conference   Springfield, AK
Co-Chair (Nominated by Faculty and Student Committee)   2007–2008

- Raised $25,000 from corporate donors, ensuring the conference met all financial obligations
- Persuaded planning committee to open the conference to neighboring colleges, resulting in a 100% increase in attendance and a 35% increase in revenue

In just two bullet points, we see evidence of the individual's successful leadership of the conference. The reader cannot doubt that this individual made wise choices and managed the conference well. For a bullet point to be most effective, it must describe both actions and results. Had these bullets related only the candidate's actions, what would they have told us about the co-chair?

- Raised $25,000 from corporate donors
- Persuaded planning committee to open the conference to neighboring colleges

We would be left wondering whether the $25,000 raised was enough and whether opening the conference to others was a good idea. With no information on the results of these actions, we are unable to determine whether the individual's efforts were in fact positive or not. We need the writer to validate his actions!

- Raised $25,000 from corporate donors, ensuring the conference met all financial obligations
- Persuaded planning committee to open the conference to neighboring colleges, resulting in a 100% increase in attendance and a 35% increase in revenue

With the addition of these critical data elements, we can now see that not only did the candidate undertake specific efforts and introduce new ideas, but also that these efforts were ultimately useful and effective—thereby demonstrating that the candidate's instincts and skills are strong with respect to these kinds of projects. The bullet points validate the actions described by offering clear results.

QUANTIFIABLE VERSUS NONQUANTIFIABLE OUT-COMES

At this point, you may be wondering, "What if my results are not quantifiable?" Although quantifiable results are preferred because they clearly convey your success in the actions you undertook, in some instances, you simply cannot measure and communicate your achievements in these kinds of terms. In such cases, you might instead demonstrate nonquantifiable results. Consider the following examples:

- Initiated a "week in review" study program that incorporated current events and academic review; program was subsequently adopted by two other IPE TAs

- Developed snowboarding product knowledge and regularly hosted "teach-ins" for 12-member staff on product attributes

In each of these sample bullets, the direct results of the candidate's actions are not measurable, but they are nonetheless important. We cannot understand the impact of the "week in review" on students in quantifiable terms, but we know it was worthwhile because other teaching assistants apparently saw the value of the program, given that they adopted the same format. Similarly, although the outcome of developing snowboarding knowledge may not be quantifiably tied to a rise in sales evidenced by a specific dollar amount, the reader still knows that the writer was effective in this position because he added value by regularly teaching others on the staff and thereby ensuring that these workers could better assist customers.

LESS OBVIOUS ACCOMPLISHMENTS

Inevitably, some JD candidates will worry that they just do not have the necessary accomplishments or results with which to build an effective résumé. For example, what can someone really say about working in basic retail or serving as a summer camp counselor or waiting tables at a restaurant? And are these kinds of positions even relevant? If you are creating your résumé at an early stage in your career, the short answer is yes—such experiences are absolutely relevant to who you are and thus to your ability to make an impression on the admissions committee. And fortunately, conveying the value of such experiences is possible with some focused effort.

To illustrate, let us revisit the retail-related entry we examined earlier, and you will see that we can learn a fair amount about the candidate:

Sports Stuff   Springfield, AK
Sales Specialist   2005–2008
- Maintained 20-hour workweek throughout the academic year, self-financing a significant portion of tuition and living expenses
- Developed snowboarding product knowledge and regularly hosted "teach-ins" for 12-member staff on product attributes

We can deduce that the candidate is dedicated to his work—and to himself—because, for three academic years, he maintained a demanding part-time schedule. We also learn that not only was he able to develop significant knowledge about the products he was selling, but he also grasped the information well enough to be qualified to teach others. In addition, this implies that he had the appropriate skills to serve in a teaching capacity and the leadership abilities necessary to host the training sessions. He may not have changed the world of sporting goods or caused a notable spike in sales, but he has two strong bullet points that speak well of him.

Please understand that we are certainly not suggesting that you embellish your accomplishments—just do not discount them! So, if you were a summer camp counselor and earned positive reviews from your supervisors, consider writing a bullet like the following:

- Planned outdoor programming for a group of 20 13-year-olds, earning top year-end reviews and an invitation to return the following season

If you were an excellent server, you might write a bullet point like the following:

- Consistently and professionally served restaurant clientele, earning the right to select among the restaurant's best shifts

Do not discount or downplay your experiences. Instead, embrace your achievements and exhibit them in the most positive light possible.

§ EXERCISE

To get you started on your résumé, we have created an exercise to simplify the area in which most applicants struggle—bullet construction. Following this exercise should make the résumé-writing process a bit easier!

Take a moment and write out a few key actions you have taken in a recent position. Try to remember to use an action verb at the beginning of each statement.

1. Action:

2. Action:

3. Action:

Now, validate these actions by describing the results of each:

1. Result:

2. Result:

3. Result:

Now, fuse these actions and results and you will have rough bullet points with which you can populate your résumé:

1. Bullet:

2. Bullet:

3. Bullet:

Repeat this exercise for each position you have held in your professional career, as well as in your extracurricular activities, if applicable.

§ NEXT STEPS

You will see two sample résumés on the following pages. The first is actually the very résumé that we constructed throughout this chapter. You can go to http://info.jdmission.com/sample-resumes to see formatted versions of these résumés. The second follows the same principles but has its own considerations based on this individual's experience (few college activities, lengthier work experience, and more).

SAMUEL P. ROOS

EDUCATION

University of XYZ   Springfield, AK

Bachelor of Arts in Political Studies, GPA 3.7   2009

Awards:

- Department Nominee, Faculty of Arts Undergraduate Student of the Year (2009)
- Recipient, Smithson Language Study Scholarship (2008)
- Recipient, Dean's List recognition (2006–2009)

PROFESSIONAL EXPERIENCE

College Franchise Painter, Inc.   Springfield, AK

Franchisee   Summers 2008, 2009

- Acquired $10,000 in "friends and family" funding to purchase franchise; paid off loans and generated an 11% return on investors' capital in 2008
- Developed marketing campaign and relationships with contractors; generated $90,000 in revenue each summer
- Hired, trained, and maintained a staff of ten college painters throughout summer; typical franchise employee turnover 20%
- Sold well-developed franchise to fellow-student for $15,000, realizing 50% return on initial franchise cost

Sports Stuff   Springfield, AK

Sales Specialist   2005–2008

- Maintained 20-hour workweek throughout the academic year, self-financing a significant portion of tuition and living expenses
- Developed snowboarding product knowledge and regularly hosted "teach-ins" for 12-member staff on product attributes

EXTRACURRICULAR ACTIVITIES

Daily XYZ'er   Springfield, AK
Sports Editor   2007–2009
- Managed a team of three sports journalists, ensuring accurate reporting and fulfillment of all deadline obligations
- Created "FANtastic sports minute" contest, generating 175 fan videos and 30,000 hits to *XYZ'er* website

Department of Political Studies   Springfield, AK
Teaching Assistant (TA), International Political Economy (IPE)   2008–2009
- Initiated a "week in review" study program, which incorporated current events and academic review; program was subsequently adopted by two other IPE TAs

Political Studies Student Conference   Springfield, AK
Co-Chair (Nominated by Faculty and Student Committee)   2007–2008
- Raised $25,000 from corporate donors, ensuring the conference met all financial obligations
- Persuaded planning committee to open the conference to neighboring colleges, resulting in a 100% increase in attendance and a 35% increase in revenue

Personal
Languages: Fluent in Spanish, conversational Arabic, conversational French
Passions: Snowboarding, walking my dog (Phil) around Springfield, Chinese cooking (completed three classes)

ALEXANDRA MORRIS

EDUCATION

Concord University, Bachelor of Commerce   Stowe, VT

Concentration: Finance and Entrepreneurship   2007–2010

Thesis: "The Asian Contagion's Effect on Minimum Wages in Vietnam and Cambodia"

PROFESSIONAL EXPERIENCE

Limestore International   Hong Kong

Analyst   Sept. 2010–Present

Limestore International is a 120-person exporting firm.

- Isolated key variables (labor, currency, raw materials) affecting product costs; analysis ultimately presented to senior management
- Created automated vendor scorecard, enabling the purchasing team to rank 35 comparable vendors (based on delivery time, quality, price), resulting in more efficient purchasing choices
- Collaborated with the IT team to identify areas of inconsistency, harmonizing processes and resolving inefficiencies within the system, saving countless man hours
- Acted as liaison between Hong Kong and U.S. offices, ensuring effective cross-cultural communications

National Electric Company   Burlington, VT

Product Coordinator – Indoor Lighting   May–Sept. 2010

National Electric is a 150-person distributor of lighting and electronic products.

- Coordinated the sourcing of new products with company's China team, leading to a significantly enhanced product line for North American clients
- Monitored market trends and identified retail customers' preferences, allowing the sales team to pitch the appropriate products to major corporate clients (Canadian Tire, Walmart, Rona, etc.)

Rosen-Crane Packaging   Waterbury, VT

Customer Service Representative   Summers 2007, 2008, 2009

Rosen-Crane is a 300-person manufacturer of corrugated boxes.

- Processed client orders and set up delivery times, ensuring on-time delivery
- Informed customers of delayed deliveries and resolved such problems
- Served hundreds of customers, making product recommendations to serve their individual needs

LEADERSHIP ACTIVITIES

Takua Pa Orphanage   Takua Pa, Thailand

Volunteer   2009

Home for children orphaned by the 2005 tsunami

- Marketed and sold handcrafted products, created by orphans, within Thai tourist industry, channeling profits to cover basic health and welfare needs
- Tutored young children in English, helping them develop basic language skills

Juvenile Diabetes Research Foundation   Stowe, VT

Young Leadership Board Member   2009–Present

- Promoted annual "Walk for the Cure," personally registering 30 walkers
- Persuaded local radio station to record commercial for the organization for free; gained free advertisement on two local radio stations

PERSONAL

- Travel: Extensive travel in South America; visited every country in Southeast Asia
- Athletics: Intramural hockey, football, and volleyball; completed Stowe Triathlon

CHAPTER 4

MAKING THE MOST OF ADDENDA

By the time you read this, the June 2011 Anthony Weiner scandal will probably be forgotten—many of you reading this will likely scratch your head and think, "I know that name from somewhere." Well, let us refresh your memory. Anthony Weiner was once a congressman on the rise, with ambitions of becoming the next mayor of New York City or attaining an even higher political position. But then Congressman Weiner sent a Tweet gone wrong to a young woman—attaching a photo of himself in his underwear, no less. Rather than immediately owning up to his error and asking for forgiveness when the Tweet was leaked to the press, however, Weiner claimed that his Twitter and yfrog accounts had been hacked and chose to constantly reassert that claim. Soon, though, his cover-up story began to unravel as other young women began to come forward to claim that they had received similar Tweets from the congressman, also with racy pictures that would prove embarrassing to the married politician. In the end, Congressman Weiner was defamed in the press, and more and more congressmen across party lines turned against him, all but forcing him to resign. Why do we feel the need to recount this sordid story for you? We believe it is a classic illustration of what can happen when someone—in this case, Congressman Weiner—fails to follow the golden rule of crisis management: "Get ahead of the scandal."

If you, as a JD candidate, have any issues in your history or profile that would warrant explanation to a law school admissions committee, you will need to follow this golden rule yourself and get ahead of your "scandal." We doubt that you have anything of the magnitude of the Anthony Weiner incident in your past—or at least we certainly hope you do not—but if you are considering hiding any element of your candidacy from your target schools, we definitely urge you to disclose it instead. Admissions officers, simply put, do not enjoy a mystery. In fact, they *hate* surprises. They ask applicants for information, and they both want and expect full disclosure. So, *disclose*. This is where addenda come into play in your law school application process.

Simply put, an addendum is a short, optional essay that you can use to explain any aberrations or negative aspects of your candidacy to the law school admissions committee. So, what kinds of situations might require an addendum? Here are a few common options:

- An undergraduate disciplinary issue

- An arrest, charges, and/or conviction

- Academic problems/issues

- A nonrepresentative LSAT score

Although the specifics of an issue will vary from candidate to candidate, properly addressing any of these situations in an addendum simply requires a certain level of honesty and directness, as we will demonstrate in detail in this chapter.

The bottom line is that almost any kind of "scandal" in your candidacy can be overcome if addressed properly. To determine whether the skeleton in your closet warrants an addendum or not, you will first need to consider the question (or questions) your target school poses. For example, Yale Law School states simply, "You may use this attachment slot to include any additional information necessary for a full representation of your candidacy," thereby offering a very broad opportunity to submit an addendum that could cover "any additional information." On the other hand, the University of Michigan Law School takes a much more narrow view, asking that you only explain instances of academic misconduct and/or criminal charges or convictions:

1. *If you answered Yes to the Conduct question "Have you ever been subject to disciplinary action for academic or other reasons in any of the colleges, universities, graduate, or professional schools you have attended, or are such charges pending or expected to be brought against you," you must submit an electronic attachment with any affirmative responses; provide complete details, including dates and resolution.*

2. *If you answered Yes to the Conduct question "Have you ever been convicted of a crime (following a jury or bench trial, a guilty plea, or a nolo contendere plea) including misdemeanors and infractions, but excluding minor traffic violations, or are such criminal charges pending or expected to be brought against you," you must submit an electronic attachment with any affirmative responses; provide complete details, including dates and resolution.*

In the end, regardless of how a school words its addenda question and what information it specifically requests, the key is properly framing the information you submit in addendum form, which we will explain in the following sections as we address how to approach these four most common kinds of "scandals."

For many, this may not need to be said, but just to be clear, the addendum is not another optional essay. It is *not* an opportunity to work in a final plug. And in fact, you are not required to write an addendum at all. This add-on to your application is the place to briefly discuss a problem and that is it!

§ Writing an Addendum about an Undergraduate Disciplinary Issue

Let us begin by offering the example of an individual with whom we worked several years ago—someone with a perfectly valid law school candidacy but who had a significant blemish on his record. We will call this candidate Fred. Fred had a competitive GPA and LSAT score, both of which were right in the sweet spot for his target schools, and he had been active in student government and on the school newspaper at his top-20 national university. He had strong references, solid summer internship experience, a unique personal statement, and several other elements in his profile that worked in his favor. Objectively speaking, Fred was a contender, except—and you were no doubt waiting for that "except"—Fred had made a big mistake when he was an undergraduate: he had helped a member of his fraternity cheat on a test, and both students were ultimately caught and brought before a disciplinary board. Fortunately, Fred was smart enough to understand that he should admit his guilt, considering that he was indeed guilty, though he was ultimately suspended from school for a semester.

If you were to meet Fred, you would probably have a difficult time believing that he could have ever made such a mistake. Maybe he caved to peer pressure from his fraternity brother. Maybe he got caught up in the moment. Maybe he just wanted to help a friend but did so (obviously) in the wrong way. None of this actually matters. Fred made a mistake, got caught, and paid a penalty for his actions. What Fred likely did not understand at the time, though, is that this mistake would follow him—that he would have a notation on his transcript forever, revealing that he was suspended for a term for academic dishonesty. So when Fred called us and asked whether he should even bother applying to law school—how could he be a defender of justice if he was already a known cheater?—and if so, how he should deal with this issue, we told him we could not *guarantee* that he would get over his "scandal," but we certainly thought it was possible.

To mitigate this blemish on his profile in the eyes of the law school admissions committees, Fred needed to write an addendum acknowledging and explaining the situation. Let us take a look at this finished addendum first, and then we will analyze it:

> *During my sophomore year at the University of ABC, I made a naïve and terribly ill-advised choice that has profoundly influenced my academic and personal life ever since. Although I could not see it then, as I look back, the foolishness I exhibited in sharing my take-home exam with a friend is obvious.*

When my professor called me into his office one week after the exam date to discuss some "irregularities" he had noted, I took responsibility for my mistake on the spot. After admitting my guilt and making a painful call to my parents, I faced a disciplinary proceeding in which I again took full responsibility for my poor choice in front of a committee of professors and peers. In the end, I was badly humbled and given a three-month academic suspension to think about my poor decision.

After I returned home to Missouri to begin my suspension, it seemed like every week another of my parents' friends or one of my cousins would come by to visit, and each one would express their surprise at seeing me at home. Over and over, I had to swallow my pride and admit that I had been suspended for academic dishonesty—that I had made a big mistake but accepted the consequences. Although some of my friends got a good chuckle at the situation, and "Boys will be boys" was a regular refrain among my parents' friends, I did not find my circumstances at all amusing. Rather, I found the situation humiliating, though it has fortunately proved life changing. To say that I now fully consider every action and choice before moving forward would be an understatement. Although I am not hesitant to make decisions, I always contemplate their possible ramifications and impact on a very profound level before moving forward.

Before we begin our analysis of this statement, let us offer an alternative version, by contrast:

When I was in college, I joined a fraternity and thereby agreed to live by a code that decreed I would always help a fraternity brother if asked—no matter what. One day, as I was completing a take-home exam, a fraternity brother who was taking the same course, but who almost never attended class, barged into my room and told me to show him what I had written. My gut reaction was to say no, and initially I resisted, but he was persistent and reminded me of our fraternity pledge to always help a brother in need. Despite my unease, and as more fraternity brothers entered my room and started to harass me, I felt compelled to hand over my exam, just to let him look over my responses. To my horror, he began to copy my work. I protested and kept repeating that we could get in trouble, but he would not listen and continued to copy my work until he had essentially duplicated my exam. I wanted to rewrite my test after that, but I had run out of time and was forced to hand in what I had already written and what had been copied.

When I went to turn in my exam, I should have told my professor about the incident with my fraternity brother and even hesitated outside his office door for a few moments, but I was just too scared about the possible consequences. I was worried that I would be accused of actively cheating, even though my fraternity brother had pressured me into letting him copy my work. (I also worried that my fraternity would consider me a "rat" and ostracize me socially.) In the end, the professor noticed the similarities in our exams, and we were both accused of cheating. Although the other student denied that he had taken part and even accused me of cheating off of him, I admitted my role in the situation and acknowledged to the disciplinary committee that I had indeed made a mistake in sharing my answers. I regret that I helped my "friend" when I clearly should not have done so, and I accepted my punishment in the form of a three-month suspension from school, though I thought the penalty was excessive. I had to return home and live with my parents for several months, which gave me plenty of time to think about how to better withstand such pressures going forward.

Take a moment and consider the differences between these two addenda. What characterizes the first example? What characterizes the second? We believe three elements in particular make one of these options much stronger than the other and deserve some closer attention: responsibility, brevity, and change.

Responsibility: In the first addendum, Fred does not even mention his fraternity or his fraternity brother. Why? Or should we ask, why *not*? The answer is that Fred knows that the admissions committee is not interested in reading an addendum about his friend or a group to which Fred belongs. Fred is writing about himself and his actions and should therefore focus on just his role in the situation. He did not have to share his exam answers with his friend. Fred was apparently immature at the time of the incident, but he has grown up since—and grown-ups do not shift the blame. Can an admissions officer trust that someone who is trying to place the blame on his friend years later is really a changed man and that his intention to be a virtuous lawyer is legitimate? Can an admissions officer have faith in the integrity of someone who calls his role in this disciplinary issue—one that led to a three-month academic suspension—"minimal"? Of course not. Mature, responsible Fred (sample addendum 1) has a chance of winning over the admissions committee despite this blemish on his record. Immature, irresponsible Fred (sample addendum 2) does not have a prayer. In short, own up to your mistakes.

In addition, as you take responsibility for your actions and decisions, do not be afraid to be brutally honest about your actions. You do not have to mercilessly beat yourself up or go overboard with self-deprecating comments, but honest language helps establish your sincerity and, somewhat ironically, your strength. To return to Fred as our example, only if he were an emotionally strong person could he call himself "naïve," his choices "ill-advised," and his subsequent experiences with his family and friends "humiliating." Mature Fred shows that he can view his situation with the distance necessary to be able to be self-critical. And immature Fred? Read the second sample addendum again and try to determine whether immature Fred uses any language that is honest. The reality is that immature Fred is focused primarily on making excuses, and in the end, this will not help his cause.

Brevity: You will notice that mature Fred's piece is just 300 words long and immature Fred's piece is more than 400 words. Although we cannot recommend a precise word count for all addenda, given that an addendum's final length will vary depending on the candidate and the particular situation discussed, keep in mind that shorter is better. Fred's addendum is better than immature Fred's for a variety of reasons, one of which is that it makes a more profound statement in fewer words. And we have even seen addenda that are half this length. Quite simply, if the issue in question does not require much explanation, then few words may be needed. You should not feel that you need to fill the page!

Remember, by the time the admissions officer who reads your application gets to your addendum, he or she will have already gone through the rest of your application and will likely have read dozens, if not hundreds, of others as well. So try to put yourself in the admissions officer's position: applications are piling up and you are doing your best to ensure that each applicant gets your full attention, but you have a lot of work ahead of you—and somewhat repetitious work at that. Our point is that by submitting an addendum, you are essentially asking the admissions officer to do even more work. Thus, the key to writing an effective addendum is to respect this individual's time and be as brief as possible while still conveying all the necessary information.

Change: Whenever you mention a failing of some kind in your addendum, do your best to reveal that you have changed as a result. Although immature Fred acknowledged in his addendum that he regretted the cheating situation and gave the incident plenty of thought during his three-month suspension, he did not discuss how he had changed because of the incident. Mature Fred, on the other hand, explained that he has a different, more mature approach to life as a result:

> *Rather, I found the situation humiliating, though it has fortunately proved life changing. To say that I now fully consider every action and choice before moving forward would be an understatement. Although I am not hesitant to make decisions, I always contemplate their possible ramifications and impact on a very profound level before moving forward.*

This is good, but what would be even better is if Fred could describe some specific actions he took after the incident that would clearly demonstrate that he has separated himself from his past and proactively taken steps to change. For example, if Fred had returned to school after his suspension and joined the honor committee or the disciplinary committee, or had chosen to enroll in additional ethics courses, or perhaps had written an essay on his experience for the school paper, he might have been able to include a passage like the following in his addendum:

> *Rather, I found the situation humiliating, though it has fortunately proved life changing. To say that I now fully consider every action and choice before moving forward would be an understatement. Although I am not hesitant to make decisions, I always contemplate their possible ramifications and impact on a very profound level before moving forward. In addition, when I returned to school, I was determined to cement these changes and volunteered to write an article about my experience for the school paper entitled "My Best Mistake." Further, I took a "Personal Leadership" course as a prelude to joining the same disciplinary committee that I had had to face. Being accepted to the committee and earning the trust of those who had once sanctioned me was greatly rewarding and symbolized for me that I had been fully welcomed back into my school's academic and social community.*

Of course, if Fred did not actually take these steps, he could not write about them in his addendum, but the point is that redemption is important. If you need to write an addendum, take time first to consider any actions you took to better the situation—or yourself—in the aftermath of the incident, and be sure to include this information in your essay to reveal how you have changed in the interim.

We have spent a lot of words here on Fred as an example. Why? Fred had about as bad a blemish on his transcript as a candidate could have, short of being expelled or imprisoned. In the end, Fred's target law schools believed that his error represented a bad blip in his story—but just that, a blip, not a fatal character flaw—and he was admitted to two top-ten law schools. Later, after passing the bar and serving as a corporate lawyer for four years, Fred applied to business school via our sister company, mbaMission. He leveraged the ethical component of the bar exam and his years as a lawyer and a trusted adviser to further reinforce those changes. He was ultimately admitted to three top-ten MBA programs and even earned a scholarship at one. Clearly, he was able to persuade others that he had changed.

§ Writing an Addendum about an Arrest, Charges, and/or Conviction

Fred's academic misadventure is, in the context of a law school application, of much the same gravity as an arrest or low-level criminal conviction—embarrassing to disclose but not impossible to overcome. If you have been arrested for underage drinking or even drunk driving, this will probably not disqualify you from getting into law school. The idea here is to keep true criminals out of law school, not people who have exercised poor judgment.

Consider the following sample addendum by a candidate who had been charged with driving under the influence:

> On December 12, 2008, I pleaded "no contest" to the charge of driving while impaired, surrendered my license, and agreed to perform 100 hours of community service. I completed those hours in three months, even though the judge had mandated a six-month time frame, volunteering with Mothers Against Drunk Driving (MADD). I continue to work with MADD to this day, speaking to school groups about my experience and helping in the local chapter's office, stuffing envelopes and completing data entry.

The Sunday I was charged, I had made the most serious error in judgment of my life by driving home after watching football at a friend's house and ingesting a number of beers. In doing so, I not only put my life—but more importantly, the lives of others—at risk. I made an awful mistake that day, but I have definitely changed and I am doing my best to make sure that others do not make the same error in judgment that I did.

Why is this addendum effective? The writer is clearly contrite and offers no histrionics. He is brief in his statement but still gets his point across. And finally, he presents evidence of his penitence, which is then reinforced by considerable proof of change indicated by his continued volunteer work. Any balanced reader should accept the writer's statement and recognize that he has matured and that this incident should in no way prevent him from being a successful JD student and ultimately an effective lawyer.

§ Writing an Addendum about an Academic Issue

Academic issues you may want to address in an addendum can vary widely, though the most common ones we have encountered deal with low grades, either a one-time instance or a set period during which the candidate performed below his or her norm academically. Is having been convicted of a crime or having been suspended worse than earning some bad grades? We would expect so, but you can never really know how the admissions committee might measure such things, so academic issues should be approached with the same level of seriousness, honesty, and directness as the other situations we have discussed thus far in this chapter. In the end, if an applicant who cheated during college can gain admission to law school, so can an applicant who let his or her grades slip momentarily. So, if you are concerned about how some aspect of your transcript or GPA could affect your candidacy, recognize first that not everyone who gets into law school had perfect grades in college, and then read on to learn how to address this issue in an addendum.

Keep in mind the key points for addenda that we have presented thus far—accept responsibility, focus on brevity, and demonstrate change. Now read the following sample addendum with these elements in mind:

> *When I was in college, I was very devoted to extracurricular activities. I was the president of my fraternity and volunteered as a Big Brother, activities that took 20 hours per week. During my freshman year, I was so busy with my fraternity that I had trouble balancing my studies, and I finished the year with a 1.9 GPA. Thereafter, I improved dramatically, and I finished my college career with a 3.3 overall. Clearly, I learned balance with time.*

What is wrong with this statement? Primarily, the candidate does not take real responsibility: he uses extracurricular involvements as an excuse for his poor academic performance and displays absolutely no soul-searching or maturity. Many individuals work to put themselves through school or are heavily involved with volunteer activities while in college yet are still able to perform at a high level academically. This person's social schedule did not prevent him from achieving academically—he prevented himself from doing so by choosing instead to spend his time away from his studies!

In contrast, consider this alternative approach:

> *My first year of college was an adjustment period for me, as anyone can clearly see from my transcript, which shows my 1.9 GPA for the year. For a brief period at the beginning of my freshman year, I mistakenly put my fraternity ahead of my academics, but thereafter, the pendulum swung the other way. Even though I took on more responsibility within my fraternity, I made sure that my classes were always my first priority. From the beginning of my sophomore year, my GPA each semester was never lower than a 3.7, and my cumulative GPA at graduation was a 3.3. I regret that the 19-year-old me left a blemish on my transcript. I feel strongly that the 3.7*

GPA I earned for six straight semesters better represents the kind of student
I truly am and ask that the admissions committee view me this way.

What works here? First, the candidate takes responsibility: he describes why his overall undergraduate GPA was lower than he felt it should be, but rather than using his membership in a fraternity as an excuse, he explains that at first, he found himself distracted from his studies but was later able to regain his focus. Second, the essay is brief—the writer does not belabor the point unnecessarily and conveys all the necessary information in less than 150 words. Third, he demonstrates change: his steady grades during his final three years at college serve as proof not only of his academic aptitude but also of his altered focus and his subsequently consistent dedication to his classes.

You may be questioning whether you really need to disclose such an issue or whether the admissions committees would even notice. The answer to both questions is "Yes!" As we discuss in Chapter 1, "What You Need to Know about Applying to Law School," admissions officers will not simply look at your overall GPA and assume this tells them everything they need to know about your entire academic history. Instead, they will look for trends and aberrations in your four-year transcript, trying to understand the deeper story behind your individual grades. As a result, they appreciate any additional information that might clarify a seemingly uncharacteristic moment or period in your college career. So, if a mystery lurks in your transcript—such as a 1.9 GPA in your first year of college followed by a 3.7 or higher each year thereafter—be sure that you tell the admissions reader that tale.

Immaturity is a simple matter of poor judgment, but sometimes a poor GPA is a matter not of judgment but of consequence. Life can throw people curveballs, and individuals often have to make the most of a challenging situation. In the following sample addendum, a candidate with a low GPA explains to the admissions committee the special circumstances behind his academic record:

My parents, neither of whom graduated from high school, never encouraged me to go to college and did not save for my education. I attended ABC University because it offered me a partial scholarship, but I still needed to work 40 hours per week to cover my remaining tuition costs and living expenses. I take great pride in the fact that I worked two eight-hour shifts at Shmuli's Furniture each weekend as an hourly salesperson, and then worked four hours three days per week as well. During my summers, I worked overtime, often as much as 60 hours per week, so I could take some of the pressure off during my academic year. I am certain that my 3.0 cumulative GPA would have been higher had I worked less and studied more, but that was simply not an option for me, and keeping my Shmuli name tag on my desk motivated me in my studies. Ultimately, I became the first in my family to earn a college degree, and I am proud that I was able to graduate debt free.

This addendum is effective because the candidate is not asking the admissions reader to feel sorry for him. In fact, he takes quite the opposite approach, expressing his pride in the sacrifices he made for the sake of his education and revealing how his job motivated him in his course work. In this case, the applicant is certainly brief but clearly takes responsibility for his choices and actions. He does not reveal that he has changed in any way, but he does not actually need to, because his dedication and character are not in question and were obviously strong from the start.

As we noted earlier, sometimes a candidate will have a primarily strong academic track record but his or her transcript includes an irregularity or aberration that is worth explaining. Let us consider the following sample addendum by an individual whose transcript shows just such an anomaly:

A quick examination of my transcript will reveal a significant aberration during my third year of college. After earning a cumulative GPA of 3.85 during my first two and a half years, I have a series of voluntary withdrawals in the second semester of my junior year. Right before that semester began, my mother was diagnosed with cancer. At her behest, I returned to school when classes began, but my mind was clearly elsewhere, and I soon withdrew from my courses and returned home. Again, with her encouragement, I returned during the summer semester in hopes of catching up on my course work and being able to graduate on time, but I quickly realized that being home to care for my mother during her treatment was too important to me. We were fortunate to discover that by the end of the summer, her chemotherapy and radiation treatments had worked and her cancer had gone into remission. I graduated just one semester late with my GPA intact, but more importantly, with my mother's health restored.

Again, this is a straightforward, credible statement of explanation, which is supported by facts. When an applicant who otherwise appears to have been a capable and committed student has this kind of aberration in his or her transcript, the admissions committee will only naturally wonder about the circumstances behind the deviation, so providing clarification via an addendum is a good idea. Again, the applicant in this case is not asking for pity but is simply explaining her circumstances, and thereby displays a level of maturity admissions committees find appealing.

We can think of almost too many possible circumstances that could affect someone's GPA, including bankruptcies, personal illnesses, originally pursuing the wrong coursework and switching majors, etc., so we cannot address them all here in this chapter. Just remember the basic keys to an effective addendum—accept responsibility, focus on brevity, and demonstrate change—and simply apply them to your specific situation.

§ Writing an Addendum about a Nonrepresentative LSAT Score

No doubt many applicants have wondered whether they should explain or justify their LSAT score to the admissions committee. When might such an addendum truly be appropriate? Note first that you should *not* write an addendum to provide an excuse for a score that you feel is lower than you had hoped. We do not need to belabor the point here, but telling the admissions committee, "I had a bad night of sleep before the test" or "There were no blinds and the sun was shining in my face so I could not concentrate" will not help you at all. With this in mind, consider the following statement:

> *During my LSAT, an air-conditioner shut down, but before it did so, it was making a continuous, loud clanking that deeply annoyed and distracted me as I was trying to complete my test. I believe that this affected my score, which is why I earned just a 161. I know that under normal circumstances, I would have scored a 165 or higher.*

By now, our "no excuses" stance should be clear. If the conditions were less than ideal in the testing center and you believe this truly had a negative impact on your final score, you can definitely appeal to the Law School Admissions Council to have your score canceled—this will not affect your chances of admission. However, you should *not* appeal to the admissions committee to give you credit that is unverifiable.

On the other hand, if you feel you put your best effort forward when you took the LSAT, yet you believe your score does not accurately represent your abilities or that some element of your score needs further clarification, you can use an addendum to explain this and hope that the admissions committee will take your reasoning into account. Ideally, you will be able to declare that you truly do have the skills necessary to succeed in law school and demonstrate evidence of these skills. Consider the following example:

> *Before graduating from college, I took the LSAT and earned a score of 161. With an offer from Bank of America's compliance group, I decided to gain some work experience before going to law school. After three years, I felt that I had the context necessary to make the most of my education. Still, with the passage of time, I felt that taking the LSAT again would be prudent. I did, and my score improved by four points, increasing to 165. I know that*

the University of ABC averages LSAT scores. In my case, because of the almost four years between tests, I would ask that you consider only my more recent score, rather than averaging the two, because I believe it is a more accurate indicator of my current abilities.

This is a straightforward, logical request for which the candidate offers a reasoned argument—the passage of several years and the evolution of his abilities during that time period. Furthermore, the statement is succinct and represents a mature, polite request.

Of course, you may find yourself in a situation in which your LSAT simply does not go well and you have no compelling backstory to help you mitigate the problem. Such a situation is unfortunate, but if your application as a whole is otherwise strong, you should still be able to demonstrate that you have something special to offer both the school and the legal profession and that you deserve a place in the class. These addenda are always challenging to write, but consider the following sample to get an idea of what an effective approach looks like:

I recognize that my LSAT score is significantly below the average for the typical ABC Law School class. I have taken the test twice, and both times, my scores have surprised and disappointed me. I have always been a strong student and was on the Dean's Honor List every semester in college. With my 3.9 GPA, I graduated in the 99th percentile of my class and earned a variety of scholarships for academic achievement, as noted in my application. I am hoping that the admissions committee will see past my LSAT score and will understand that I am a dedicated and successful academic at heart—one who will thrive amid the challenges of law school.

This addendum works because it serves as a concentrated reminder of the writer's numerous academic strengths—all of which stand in direct opposition to his disappointing LSAT score. If this candidate had an even higher GPA, had completed research for a professor, or could offer any number of other superlative accomplishments—the more evidence of his academic excellence, the better—his argument would be even stronger. In this case, the applicant has only his grades and the related recognitions (Dean's List, scholarships) to present and simply makes his case with these as his evidence. As we have seen in the other examples of effective addenda in this chapter, the candidate does not beg, plead, or make excuses.

An addendum can be a useful and powerful tool in your law school application process, allowing you to communicate directly with the admissions committee about any issues that you think might detract from your profile. Remember, however, that an addendum is not a cure-all. It cannot guarantee that you will overcome whatever obstacle you are explaining and be accepted to your target school. However, it certainly provides an opportunity to address problems or weaknesses, so that the admissions committee has complete information as it makes its decision.

CHAPTER 5

EARNING A COMPELLING LETTER OF RECOMMENDATION

"Sally was the best student I have ever had! You will be so lucky to have her in your class! She will make a fantastic lawyer. You have nothing but my unconditional recommendation. She is smart and kind and courteous. She is a well-rounded, community-minded person, in addition to being a scholar. I have many more superlatives, but it would just get repetitive. Admit Sally!"

Oh, so much is woefully wrong with this recommendation excerpt that we hardly know where to begin. In this chapter, we will pick these sentences apart, and the lessons we will present should help you properly prepare and educate your recommenders and ensure that your recommendations pack the desired punch. But before we begin our critiques, we should first ask a very basic question: Why do schools even ask for recommendations?

Every element of your law school application, including your GPA and your LSAT score, is part of a complex story that you are presenting to the admissions committee, and you have ultimate control over all of these elements *except one*—your recommendations. Your recommendations allow your target school to learn about you through *someone else's* eyes. Through your recommendations, the admissions committee hopes to gain new insight into your candidacy and will use this largely qualitative input to form a more complete picture of you and to better assess your relative value (more on that later) as a student.

A significant benefit of your recommendations is that your recommenders can write about you in a way that you cannot and can praise you, backed by evidence (more on that later, too!), in a way you cannot as well. However, your recommenders can also take you down a notch, so to speak, by exposing weaknesses or other gaps in your candidacy that you had hoped to keep hidden, so these letters can carry some level of risk. This is why properly choosing, preparing, and communicating with your recommenders is so important.

At the end of this chapter, we present a full-length sample recommendation letter that follows the guidelines we will discuss here, and we will use excerpts from this letter to illustrate our advice at several points. (You may want to take a moment now to read this letter in its entirety to gain additional context as you read this chapter.)

§ How Many Recommendations You Need

Typically, top law schools give you the option of submitting up to four letters of recommendation, as shown in Table 1. This definitely does not mean, however, that you should always provide the maximum number. Similarly, if a school gives you the opportunity to submit no recommendations at all, as Berkeley Law does, you should not forgo the opportunity to offer at least one.

For most law schools, you should plan to submit two recommendations from academics who know you well. If you have two such individuals who are willing to write letters on your behalf and you also know a professional supervisor or community leader whose recommendation could add a new window into your profile, you should go ahead and ask this person for a third letter of recommendation. We struggle to think of a time when adding a fourth letter of recommendation to your application would truly be beneficial, however.

Table 1. Recommendation Minimums and Maximums for Top Law Schools

Law School	Minimum # of Recommendations	Maximum # of Recommendations
Berkeley Law	–	4
Univ. of Chicago Law School	2	4
Columbia Law School	2	4
Harvard Law School	2	4
Univ. of Michigan Law School	1	4
New York Univ. School of Law	1	4

Univ. of Pennsylvania Law School	2	4
Stanford Law School	2	4
Univ. of Virginia School of Law	2	4
Yale Law School	2	4

Source: Data retrieved from www.lsac.org in February 2012.

§ DETERMINING WHO SHOULD WRITE YOUR RECOMMENDATIONS

Content and approach are certainly important in your recommendations, but who is doing the writing is likewise important. The opinions of certain individuals can in fact carry more weight with the admissions committees than those of others, and various traits can render some people either wonderful or troublesome recommenders, so choosing wisely is key.

We will assume that you are reading this book with significant time left before you plan to submit your completed application, in which case you have a great opportunity now to fully contemplate and do some background work on your possible recommenders to make sure your choices are indeed "safe." After all, if you play by the strictest interpretation of the rules of recommendations, you will not get to see what your recommenders write about you before they submit their letters to the school. So, by doing a little intelligence work now, you can better understand whether you are making the right choice before you commit to a certain individual.

By doing "intelligence work," we mean doing whatever possible—in a discreet and diplomatic way, of course—to learn about your potential recommenders' style and history with such tasks. For example, if any of your former classmates/colleagues have applied to law school themselves and called upon one of your possible recommenders for a letter, you should contact them to find out what their experiences were like. Was the recommender a generous advocate or a disinterested third party who had a tendency to be harsh? Did the recommender follow directions and adhere to set deadlines or seriously delay or complicate the submission process? Clearly, learning more about your target recommender's approach in advance can help you understand whether or not you should offer this person this important responsibility. Past classmates and colleagues can also guide you in how best to *manage* your recommenders, which can be just as important as choosing them. Knowing up front that your recommender is a procrastinator or performed better after being given a list of accomplishments from which to work can help ensure the best letter possible and can prevent you from inadvertently antagonizing your recommender or delaying the process.

PROFESSORS

Law school is immensely challenging and requires that students quickly digest and comprehend huge amounts of information. Law schools want to know that you have both the raw intellectual horsepower and the will necessary to handle the rigors of this kind of curriculum. For many applicants, their college experience provides the best evidence that they can indeed manage the stresses and challenges of pursuing a JD. If one of your college professors knows you well and can, you believe, write a thorough and thoughtful letter about your academic strengths, then this individual should be your first choice. A second recommendation from a professor who likewise knows you well would also be advisable.

SUPERVISORS

If your professional supervisor has managed you in a research, writing, or analytical capacity, he or she is an option for you as you contemplate recommenders. For example, if you spent several years as a legislative analyst on Capitol Hill, then your chief of staff or your congressman could offer a compelling letter discussing a number of attributes your target law school would want to read about, such as an ability to quickly understand and analyze legislation and its impacts. Similarly, if you worked in a psychology lab after graduating, running experiments and analyzing results for a professor, then you could certainly approach that professor for an appropriate recommendation letter, even if you were never a student in his or her classroom and you were paid for your work. However, if you have spent the past few years running a restaurant, you should do your best to track down a professor (who remembers you and your work, of course!) to provide your recommendation. Even if you have managed the restaurant effectively, steadily growing its revenue and profit, your supervisor in this situation will not be in a position to discuss your raw intellectual horsepower, which is what the schools want to learn about. If your supervisor can only convey stories about your character, but not your ability to hit the books and quickly assimilate dense information, he or she should not be one of your two primary references. Instead, such a supervisor would make a great third reference, because this individual is able to offer supplemental information that may not be available to those who knew you solely in the academic sphere.

If you find that you really have no choice but to ask a supervisor from your professional life to write a letter on your behalf as one of your two primary recommendations, you will need to coach this individual to make the most of this suboptimal (but not disastrous) situation. Providing this supervisor with a "cheat sheet," as we discuss later in this chapter, will significantly increase the likelihood that he or she will write a compelling and effective recommendation on your behalf.

COMMUNITY LEADERS

Similar to situations in which you might solicit a professional recommendation, you should only ask a community leader for one of your two letters of recommendation in very specific circumstances, because again, these individuals will most often not be able to effectively discuss the skills an admissions officer wants to learn about—namely, your ability to understand and analyze large amounts of information. If you want to earn your JD because you want to work as a transactional attorney, for example, you should not ask for a recommendation letter from the president of the baseball league for which you volunteer coach, because youth baseball and corporate law have no obvious connection. Your league president would not be able to provide any insight into the aspects of your personality and skills that would relate to your law school experience or goals, so his or her recommendation would prove less than useful to the admissions committee.

However, if you spent time volunteering at a domestic violence shelter and have aspirations to work as a legal aid lawyer specializing in family law, you should ask the shelter's executive director for a third recommendation, because this person *can* speak to your passion for and commitment to the field and thus lend weight to your candidacy.

You Yourself

A common response law school candidates encounter when they approach potential recommenders is "You write it and I will sign it." Some may see this as a golden opportunity to create a letter that says exactly what they want it to and nothing that they do not, but it most definitely is not. Quite simply, you should *never* agree to write your own recommendation. A primary reason is that doing so is unethical—not only wrong to begin with, but particularly inappropriate for someone embarking on a career meant to uphold truth and justice.

Another reason is that you lack the objectivity necessary to be able to identify and truly understand all the nuances of your experiences and personality. The benefit of recommendation letters—and the reason schools request them—is that they provide new and additional insight into your capabilities and experiences that you cannot offer yourself. Writing an objective, self-aware letter highlighting your own strengths can be very difficult, as can revealing aspects of your personality that have not yet been highlighted in your essays or elsewhere in your profile. In short, you will miss a lot that is interesting about you, whereas your chosen third party is much less likely to do so. Resist the temptation to write your own letter and instead offer as much help and support as possible—become your recommender's coach, not his or her ghostwriter.

§ Keys to an Effective Recommendation

As you carefully consider your options for recommenders, try to determine which ones you believe are savvy or coachable enough to follow the advice in this section. You want to avoid—at all costs—having someone write a recommendation for you like the "Sally" one we presented at the beginning of this chapter. But what exactly is wrong with that sample recommendation? What guidelines should recommenders follow to produce a more effective letter?

Focus on the Specifics

Aside from Sally's overwhelming and unconditional awesomeness (note the sarcasm!), what exactly stands out about her, based on the information provided in these few sentences? If you were to think back right now to the statements you read about Sally at the beginning of this chapter, what would you remember about her? Anything at all? Does the blurb create an image for you of who Sally is and what she has accomplished? Many recommenders mean well and truly believe they are doing the applicant a big favor by using superlatives throughout their letters and by offering emphatic (almost euphoric!) praise. However, the end result, as this sample recommendation about Sally demonstrates, is most often a letter that is so broad and devoid of useful information that it is essentially meaningless. The reader does not gain a window into who Sally is and what she can offer, because in truth, nothing specific is ever said about her.

A telling way of proving this is to replace Sally's name in the recommendation with that of any other candidate—even your own!—and the statement would still work (assuming both candidates were equally "awesome," of course). A "fill in the name" recommendation, no matter how positive, will lack impact and will thus contribute nothing in your quest to gain admission to your target law school. By contrast, consider the following excerpt from the sample recommendation letter we present in full later in this chapter:

> *In this seminar, I offer my students specific topics on which to write a 20-page paper and then lead a one-hour discussion to "launch" our in-class analysis of the topic. Braden approached me after our first session and asked if he could identify and present a topic of his own. I, of course, was delighted that he had the intellectual curiosity and the willingness to take such a risk. In my six years of teaching this course, only two other students have ever asked to present on their own topics.*

In these sentences, could you easily insert your name in place of Braden's? Did you take a seminar and ask to present on your own topic? Although we imagine this is technically possible, it is highly unlikely that you did. You might identify a coincidence or two, but your story cannot possibly match Braden's experience line for line, because it is uniquely his. In addition, Braden's recommender is not merely praising him, he is qualifying his praise with details and anecdotes. That Braden is praiseworthy is a logical conclusion anyone would draw after reading about his actions.

We will discuss how to best educate and prepare your recommenders on the evaluation process later in this chapter. For now, remember that an important aspect of any recommendation is ensuring that your recommender writes about you anecdotally, because this will bring color and life to your profile in the eyes of the admissions committee. Consider, for example, the following sample passage about Braden:

> *Braden explored a variety of important themes in his work. He challenged himself always and brought forth ideas that many others might not have considered. He was careful to think through new angles and attack prob-*

lems in many ways. In the end, his analysis was exceptional and impressive, because no stone was left unturned.

Although this example includes no shortage of praise and positive statements about Braden's performance, this would actually be considered a "weak" recommendation statement, because the admissions reader cannot conclude or see for him- or herself that Braden acted in an exceptional way—the reader has only the recommender's word. The ideas presented in these few sentences are so vague as to be unmemorable. Braden could be studying any topic, and the reader has no idea how he challenged himself, which angles he considered that others might have missed, which issues he addressed, or any other specifics about his work. Consider now, by contrast, the following excerpt:

Although many of my students tend to limit their analysis to just one or two areas, Braden considered a variety of economic, military, social, governmental, intergovernmental, and cultural issues that could lead the region to conflict. In particular, his inclusion of cultural issues was a welcome surprise—typically, students will offer a valid analysis of an issue, but they fail to take their analysis a step further and truly delve into the subtleties and nuances of a situation the way Braden did. He managed to enter the mindset of the "man on the ground," and thus revealed a level of thoughtfulness and consideration of the issues that I simply do not see in these classes.

Although we are examining this excerpt here without the full context of the entire recommendation letter, we can still easily understand from these few sentences that Braden completed a multidisciplinary study of a topic and that he considered specific cultural issues that most other students overlook. Thus, the claim that was made in the first example—that Braden's analysis was "exceptional"—is confirmed and supported in the second example through the inclusion of anecdotal details that reveal *how* his work was indeed exceptional. Instead of unqualified enthusiasm, we have a fully supported example, which is as close as we can get to proof!

PRESENT PRAISE IN RELATIVE TERMS

Your recommender does not need to be your cheerleader, singing your praises and pushing you forward regardless of your actions, but rather should be your dispassionate, objective advocate. But can anyone truly be a dispassionate, objective advocate? Would that not be a contradiction in terms? Not really. Your recommenders can use facts rather than superlatives to prove their points, and to further emphasize and illustrate their arguments about your standout qualities, they can present your achievements and attributes in relative terms. By this we mean that by explaining how they believe your behavior is distinct from—and ideally superior to—that of others, your recommenders can provide more compelling evidence that you are an exceptional candidate. Again, consider the following excerpt:

> *In this seminar, I offer my students specific topics on which to write a 20-page paper and then lead a one-hour discussion to "launch" our in-class analysis of the topic. Braden approached me after our first session and asked if he could identify and present a topic of his own. I, of course, was delighted that he had the intellectual curiosity and the willingness to take such a risk. In my six years of teaching this course, only two other students have ever asked to present on their own topics.*

Nothing in this excerpt directly states that Braden is exceptional, yet his excellence is made clear through the writer's description of how Braden performed in a way that differentiated him from other students. By simply sharing how Braden did something that his peers do not do—in this case, picked his own seminar topic, which only two other students have ever offered to do in the teacher's six-year history with the course—the instructor leads the reader to the natural conclusion that Braden is exceptional. He does not need to say so, because Braden's performance alone proves it. Wherever possible, your recommender should draw distinctions between you and others. Elite schools want elite talent—they want the person who stands out!

MAINTAIN THE PROPER FRAME OF REFERENCE

A common adage in writing is "write what you know," and this is particularly applicable to recommendations. Unless your writer has profound experience with the law or with law school, he or she should not comment on your potential abilities as a lawyer, plain and simple. So, unless they have direct experience as lawyers, judges, or legal academics, your recommenders should refrain from trying to predict your performance as a law school student or as a lawyer after graduation. Their opinion does not really matter in this regard, and more importantly, it could at worst be somewhat irritating to the educated admissions reader or simply a waste of time and words. Overwhelmingly, your recommenders should write about the past—not the future—and always from their own frame of reference.

Further, your recommenders should keep in mind that they have a certain scope of experience with you. Even though we recommend that you sit down with your recommenders and remind them of your accomplishments, your recommenders are not your biographers. They should only write about the aspects of your profile with which they actually have experience! Recall that in the excerpt at the beginning of this chapter, the writer—Sally's history professor—says that Sally is a "well-rounded, community-minded person." Not only does he not present any evidence to back up this claim, as we have already discussed, but he is also presuming to talk about an element of Sally's life in which he is not directly involved. As her professor, how would he know enough about her community activities to be able to comment appropriately on them? He should instead restrict his observations and commentary to the elements of Sally's life about which he is knowledgeable. By doing so, he would produce a much stronger and more valid recommendation (in part because he would be able to include specific examples and details) while also not wasting space on topics about which he cannot speak knowingly.

In the full sample letter we present at the end of this chapter, the recommender discusses Braden's role on the professor selection panel, which is an activity in which Braden engages *outside* the classroom. At first glance, then, this might seem outside the recommender's scope of reference. However, in this case, Braden's recommender happens to also be a member of the committee in question and has therefore been able to observe Braden's performance—his comments about it are therefore both appropriate and effective. Your recommenders should not try to learn about your outside pursuits to be able to discuss them in their letters, either. Instead, they should refamiliarize themselves with the particular experiences they have shared with you or observed directly and then focus on writing about what they truly know.

PERSUADE RATHER THAN CAMPAIGN

Just as your recommenders should not try to act like your cheerleaders, they should not use their letters to campaign for your acceptance into law school. Your recommendations are meant to inform the admissions reader about your strengths and accomplishments from an outsider's point of view, not to coax or cajole the reader into admitting you. In other words, the caliber of your profile should be what compels the admissions committee to grant you an acceptance letter—not a third party's fancy writing. Your recommendation letters should therefore not include statements like "Admit Sally!" or "I implore you to find a place for this excellent student in your class. You will be rewarded for this choice!"

The admissions reader is not going to be swayed by a simple, jingoistic approach and is likely to be annoyed by your recommender's obvious lack of balance. As you will note while reading through the sample recommendation letter at the end of this chapter, the author clearly wants the admissions committee to "admit Braden," but he never directly states this. Quite simply, he does not need to, because he has instead described Braden as obviously deserving in his own right. The implication behind the recommender's positive representation of Braden's accomplishments and unique qualities—and behind the recommender's willingness to write such a letter on Braden's behalf in the first place—is that the recommender believes that Braden is an exceptional student worthy of law school admittance. Your recommenders should relay anecdotes in a meaningful way, not implore the reader to admit you or try to rouse him or her to action. Ironically, the most powerful recommendation letters are those that are most subtly persuasive.

§ COACHING YOUR RECOMMENDERS

Once you have identified your intended recommenders, definitely take the time to meet with each of them and discuss the advice outlined in the previous section *before* they begin writing your letters. This is a vitally important step, and one most candidates do not think to take. You can even remind your recommenders about stories involving them that could be beneficial to include in the letters they will write.

Reviewing your accomplishments and contributions with your recommenders is perfectly ethical. After all, you are simply refreshing their memory about factual events and about your personal strengths; you are not telling them what to write or doing the writing for them. By sitting down with your recommenders and reviewing your accomplishments with them, you ensure that relevant material about you is fresh in their minds.

Successfully coaching your recommenders involves four key steps:

1. Formally request a recommendation

2. Discuss the nature of the letter/recommendation

3. Manage deadlines

4. Provide a "cheat sheet" of accomplishments

FORMALLY REQUEST A RECOMMENDATION

At this point, we hope we have sufficiently made our point about the importance of your recommendation letters. With this in mind, you should not just casually ask your chosen recommender to write a letter for you whenever you happen to see him or her. Instead, arrange a time to meet with each of your target recommenders one-on-one to discuss the issue at hand with their full attention. During this meeting, you should be able to gauge how wholeheartedly your recommender can back your candidacy, and therefore whether you should proceed with asking for a recommendation. For example, if your target recommender says, "I am a bit busy right now. You may want to ask someone else," you should not persist; this is essentially a polite way of saying, "I do not want to be your advocate," so you will need to look elsewhere for a recommendation you can trust. Most of the time, your chosen recommender will provide clues that subtly, but clearly, indicate how enthusiastically he or she can support you. Watch for these clues and, as appropriate, either move forward with your recommendation request or politely thank the individual for his or her time and move on to the next potential recommender on your list.

DISCUSS THE NATURE OF THE RECOMMENDATION

In general, you should emphasize to all your recommenders that the application process for law school is a competitive one and that you do not need them to brag on your behalf, but to write about you in a manner that clearly differentiates you from the rest of the pack. Keep in mind—and diplomatically share with your recommenders—the four keys to an effective recommendation that we presented earlier in this chapter:

- *Focus on the specifics*: Explain to your recommenders that they should confirm and support their positive declarations about you and your performance by including detailed anecdotes that reveal *how* you or your work is indeed exceptional. Be sure to also explain what a "fill in the name" recommendation is and let your recommenders know that no matter how positive such a letter might seem, it will actually lack impact and thus contribute nothing to help you gain admission to your target law school.

- *Present praise in relative terms*: Discuss with your recommenders the relative differences between you and others, and try to identify and share with them a few ways in which you stand out in a directly comparative manner.

- *Maintain the proper frame of reference*: Discourage, if you must, your recommenders from trying to learn about your outside pursuits to be able to comment on them in their letters, and explain that they should refamiliarize themselves with the particular experiences they have shared with you or observed directly and focus on writing about what they truly know.

- *Persuade rather than campaign*: Ask your recommenders to relay anecdotes in a meaningful way, not to implore the reader to admit you or to rouse him or her to action.

Manage Deadlines

When you meet with your recommenders, be prepared to set a deadline by which you, or the school, will need the finished letter. You may feel that you are already asking these individuals for an important favor and therefore should not be "pushy" by imposing a deadline, but this is a mistake, and you have no real reason to feel shy about broaching the subject of a set end date. Moreover, writing recommendation letters is actually part of the job of a professor or supervisor. You should be diplomatic and up front in your request, of course—"I am expecting to submit my application in early October. Would you have time between now and then to write my letter?"—but discussing a deadline for the letter is not only appropriate, it is necessary to ensure your complete application can be submitted on your schedule.

PROVIDE A "CHEAT SHEET" OF ACCOMPLISHMENTS

At this point, you have formally requested a recommendation, discussed effective approaches, and set a submission deadline, which are all important components of this process, but informing and reminding your recommenders of specific information they could include in their letters may be the most crucial step of all. During your meetings with your recommenders, be sure to refresh their memories with respect to your accomplishments and progress. Briefly share your reasons for pursuing a JD, your reasons for choosing the schools you are targeting, and your ambitions for after graduation.

Most importantly, leave your recommenders with a written list—what we call a "cheat sheet"—of accomplishments that occurred directly under their supervision. Such a document not only serves to remind your recommenders of significant high points in your academic or professional career to date (and may even lead them to remember other achievements you forgot or overlooked yourself), but it also helps them more easily include key examples and details in their finished letters. Moreover, in our experience, we have found that far from feeling that you are being pushy in providing this kind of document, virtually all recommenders appreciate this kind of guidance.

A sample cheat sheet and a full corresponding recommendation letter follow.

SAMPLE "CHEAT SHEET"

Braden Hillman

Political Studies Student/Law School Applicant

Academic Accomplishments

- Dean's List each semester
- 3.91 GPA
- Wilson Entrance Scholarship ($5,000 per year)
- Jonathan Robertson Award (Best freshman political essay—one of four winners)

"Transnational Conflict Resolution" Course

- Selected own seminar topic—"A Day Late and a Million Gallons Short: Water Problems in East Africa"
- Volunteered to present first, among 12 students
- Critiqued Jonas Kay's paper "More Weapons Now: The New Case for Nuclear Deterrence"
- Consistent class participant; always respectful of others' efforts; made sure to fully read classmates' papers before class and to formulate questions (I recognize that this is not a heroic achievement, but many did not provide this courtesy)
- Earned the highest grade in the class

"Studies in Global Political Economy" Course

- Lobbied you and department to enter this graduate-level class
- Only undergraduate student in graduate class; earned an A
- Presented my own topic regarding how intellectual property development in the West is destroying property

rights in developing nations ("Intellectual Property Wrongs: The Destructive Effects of Innovation on the Developing World"); deemed "radical" by classmates

Departmental Commitments: Professor Hiring Committee

- Was invited to serve as an undergraduate student member

- Full committee member; was not afraid to voice opinions

- Huge commitment of hours to select new professors

- Ultimately, the department is better off for these hires

Recommendation Submission Deadline is October 31, 201X

Credential Assembly Service's Instructions for recommender:

The person whose name appears above is applying to one or more Credential Assembly Service–participating law schools. This applicant has requested a letter of recommendation from you, and it would be very helpful if you submit your signed letter as soon as possible. Law schools value your candid appraisal of the applicant's ability, academic and otherwise, to study law, including qualities of mind and character, dedication, responsibility, and readiness for the rigors of advanced academic study. Evidence of overcoming adversity, rising to challenges, and achieving beyond expectations is helpful in assessing candidates for admission. You may wish to include how well you know the candidate and in what capacity, your assessment of the relative strength of the candidate within the reference group in which she or he is being compared, and how the candidate will add to the diversity of the law school.

SAMPLE RECOMMENDATION LETTER

As a professor of political science at EFG College, I am given considerable latitude in structuring my classes. I teach one undergraduate class and one graduate class each year, both of which meet throughout the academic year for three hours per week. I keep my class sizes at a maximum of 12 students to encourage interaction and participation, and as such, I have the opportunity for significant interaction with my students. Braden Hillman took each of my seminar classes—notably taking my graduate-level course while still an undergraduate student—and during this time I got to know him quite well. I am confident in my ability to discuss his attributes and recommend him to ABC Law School.

In my undergraduate class, "Transnational Conflict and Resolution," Braden distinguished himself among his peers through his scholarship and through his approach to others' work. In an undergraduate seminar class, where students earn a significant portion of their grades through participation, some students frequently mistake academic contribution with merely speaking in class. Braden was thoughtful in what he said—never needlessly provocative, as many undergraduates can be—and was always sensitive to the viewpoints of others, whether he was diplomatically disagreeing or being undiplomatically disagreed with. He was one of the first students to lead a classroom discussion and did so with an hour-long dissection of potential conflicts due to water shortages in East Africa. I recall being impressed by two elements in particular:

1. *Braden selected his own seminar topic: In this seminar, I offer my students specific topics on which to write a 20-page paper and then lead a one-hour discussion to "launch" our in-class analysis of the topic. Braden approached me after our first session and asked if he could identify and present a topic of his own. I, of course, was delighted that he had the intellectual curiosity and the willingness to take such a risk. In my six years teaching this course, only two other students have ever asked to present on their own topics.*

Clearly, this type of maturity and confidence is rare at the undergraduate level and suggested to me that I had a serious student on my hands, one who had the maturity to test himself.

2. *Braden's analysis of the problem was multidisciplinary in nature: Although many of my students tend to limit their analysis to just one or two areas, Braden considered a variety of economic, military, social, governmental, intergovernmental, and cultural issues that could lead the region to conflict. In particular, the inclusion of cultural issues was a welcome surprise— typically, students will offer a valid analysis of an issue, but they fail to take their analysis a step further and truly delve into the subtleties and nuances of a situation the way Braden did. Braden managed to enter the mind-set of the "man on the ground," and thus revealed a level of thoughtfulness and consideration of the issues that I simply do not see in these classes. Because of this added level of analysis, I awarded Braden the highest grade in the class on his seminar paper and ultimately the highest grade in the class at the end of the course.*

After the "Transnational Conflict Resolution" class, Braden again showed initiative and maturity by asking to take part in my graduate class, "Studies in Global Political Economy." It is worth noting that he not only had to prevail upon me to gain a place in the class, but he also had to persuade the head of our department that he could handle the work. Braden entered this class with first- and second-year graduate students without any ego. His approach to seminars had not changed—he did not feel that he needed to be heard and judiciously chose his times to contribute. Again, he asked to present his own topic—this time it was "Intellectual Property Wrongs: The Destructive Effects of Innovation on the Developing World"—and completed a rigorous analysis that withstood the questioning of those with more years of scholarship. Although Braden did not earn the highest grade in this class, he still earned an A grade and certainly rewarded us for our willingness to make an exception in admitting him.

Because Braden had earned the respect of his peers and the faculty, he was invited to be the undergraduate student representative on the college's Professor Hiring Committee, of which I am also a member. Braden volunteered his time, alongside a graduate student and five professors, in evaluating hundreds of CVs, interviewing ten candidates, listening to three lectures, and then aggregating and evaluating these candidates. It is clearly a testament to his maturity that he was selected, and Braden approached the process with exemplary professionalism and care for the department's future. Braden's commitment of hours was enormous, but his focus never wavered and his academics never suffered. Ultimately, we made an important hiring decision, and Braden's equal vote was counted—his presence was felt on the panel.

Braden has already outperformed his peers and proven that he can manage graduate coursework. As I have noted, he has the maturity and thoughtfulness necessary to earn others' respect and to make valuable contributions in the classroom. He is a curious individual who takes his academics seriously and will no doubt continue to thrive with new academic challenges.

Should you have any questions at all, please do not hesitate to call me: (8X7) X45-X67X.

A Note on Evaluations

Some law schools may give you the opportunity to have your recommender (or a different person, if you so choose) complete an evaluation form about you instead of or in addition to submitting a letter of recommendation. This is a somewhat new option for students and schools, and the evaluation has not yet gained widespread acceptance. In fact, of the top-ten law schools, as ranked by *U.S. News & World Report* (2011), not one requires candidates to submit an evaluation. Of them, Berkeley Law, Columbia Law School, Harvard Law School, and the University of Virginia School of Law will not accept an evaluation at all. Meanwhile, the University of Chicago Law School, the University of Michigan Law School, the New York University School of Law, the University of Pennsylvania Law School, Stanford Law School, and Yale Law School make evaluations an option.

Most candidates consider evaluations "devalued" because many schools will not accept them yet. Nonetheless, in *rare* circumstances, some recommenders may find evaluations helpful, particularly if they find they are having difficulty structuring their ideas or effectively presenting their thoughts in the traditional recommendation format. For most, however, completing an evaluation may actually require more work, because they will need to write comments for six different sections (as we will explain) and complete a free-form section at the end. You want to avoid burdening your evaluators, so please be cautious in venturing down this path!

Via a standardized form, your evaluator will be asked to assess your skills, abilities, and character in the following six areas:

1. Communication

2. Integrity and honesty

3. Intellectual skill

4. Personal qualities

5. Task management

6. Working with others

Within each of these sections, your evaluator will be asked to respond to a number of questions using the following ranking options and to identify the peer group within which he or she is rating you (e.g., your classmates, your coworkers, etc.):

- Average (Top 50%)

- Good (Top 25%)

- Very Good (Top 10%)

- Excellent (Top 5%)

- Truly Exceptional (Top 1%–2%)

- Inadequate Opportunity to Judge

For example, then, in the "Personal qualities" section of the evaluation, your evaluator would be presented with the following statements and asked to assess how each statement applies to you using the quantitative percentage delineations we have just presented:

- Is highly motivated

- Shows empathy and compassion

- Has surmounted difficulties and obstacles

- Possesses practical judgment

- Shows initiative

- Demonstrates professionalism

So, your evaluator would see an entry like the following:

Is highly motivated

- ◯ Below Average (Bottom 50%)
- ◯ Average (Top 50%)
- ◯ Good (Top 25%)
- ◯ Very Good (Top 10%)
- ◯ Excellent (Top 5%)
- ◯ Truly Exceptional (Top 1%–2%)
- ◯ Inadequate Opportunity to Judge

After responding to all the questions in each category, your evaluator would then see the following statement:

Please add any comments that would help clarify your rating:

Over and over, your evaluator will be required to answer questions—30 in all—ranking you within the various categories we have outlined, and will then need to write additional comments to clarify his or her ratings in each section. Because evaluations can be rather demanding in this way, and because you do not want your evaluator to be caught off guard when asked to clarify or qualify his or her ratings, if you choose this recommendation option, you must be sure to prepare this individual for the demands of the form and motivate him or her to think about your relative strengths before completing the evaluation.

Law schools do not want the top 25%—they want the elite. The entire evaluation is about *relative* strengths, and your evaluator will not only need to give you consistently high ratings, he or she will need to adequately *justify* those ratings. Here and there your recommender can offer a slightly lower rating for balance and to ensure believability (no candidate will likely be exceptional across the board), but overwhelmingly, your recommender will need to rate you highly and back the rating up with examples (i.e., provide evidence!).

For the "highly motivated" sample question we presented earlier, Braden's recommender would have no trouble offering adequate context and convincing evidence to support a high ranking:

Please add any comments that would help clarify your rating:

I have ranked Braden Hillman as truly exceptional with respect to his motivation because in the six years I have taught my seminar, he was one of only three individuals who elected to identify his own topic to present. Not only did I appreciate his ambition, but Braden also came through with a very well-researched paper that approached the problem at hand in a far more complex and mature way than I had expected. He considered a depth of angles—economic, cultural, political, etc.—in his analysis, whereas others in the past have only considered one. This obviously required motivation. He pushed himself to do a far more thorough job than others and, as a reward, earned the highest grade in the class.

In reading this chapter, you may suddenly realize that actively *managing* your recommenders—rather than simply asking them nicely for assistance and hoping for the best—is crucial in maximizing the impact of this application component. Before you visit your recommenders, reread this section and prepare appropriately for your meetings with them. Some simple organization on your part should result in more effective recommendations when an admissions officer sits down to read your file.

CHAPTER 6

EFFECTIVE INTERVIEW TECHNIQUES

Have you ever heard a joke about a lawyer? You must have—everyone has. Lawyers hate them, of course, because by and large, lawyers are actually an honorable crew. They do not find having their integrity impugned particularly funny. (Would you?) Still, largely unjustly, negative stereotypes persist about the ethics and motives of those in the legal profession. Because of this image problem, we would assume that law schools would want to protect the reputation of the profession they support and be as thorough as possible in interviewing all candidates to weed out any possible "bad apples," right?

The answer is... not really. By and large, law schools actually do *not* interview their applicants. Candidates (almost always) submit online applications and then wait a few weeks or months to learn whether they have been accepted to or rejected by their target schools. That is it in a nutshell. Business schools and medical schools, on the other hand, almost never accept candidates into their programs without first interviewing them. These days, many high-end preschools even interview toddlers! Yet for some reason, law schools continue to buck the trend.

§ THE AVAILABILITY OF INTERVIEWS

Top law schools generally take one of four approaches to interviews, which we categorize in order from most to least popular, as follows:

1. No interviews at all

2. Invitation-only interviews

3. As-needed interviews

4. Open interviews

Later in this chapter, we discuss in more depth the various reasons schools choose to interview applicants.

No Interviews at All

You may be surprised to learn that few law schools feel that interviewing anyone at all is necessary. We tend to think of this as the "We won't interview you or anyone else, period. Leave us alone. Thank you." view. We suppose this lack of an interview could be the admissions office's testament to the law school experience—they are reading your files and assimilating all necessary information without other direct input, just as you will have to do with your case studies. More likely, though, it is a matter of resources.

In fact, on their websites, many schools explicitly reference their lack of resources to explain why they do not offer interviews, and indeed, the resources required in most cases would no doubt be overwhelming. Northwestern Law, the only leading law school that is open to interviewing all its applicants, interviews almost 3,700 candidates each year to yield a class of approximately 265 students. Considering that each interview lasts roughly half an hour, Northwestern staff would need to dedicate 1,850 hours per year—almost the equivalent of one full-time staff member's time for an entire year—just to complete the interviews themselves. Note that this does *not* include the time needed for pre-interview scheduling and preparation, for post-interview write-ups, or for reviewing these interviews late in the admissions decision-making process. So, we can probably take the following schools at their word when they claim to not have the resources necessary to be able to commit to interviewing all applicants:

> *The large number of applicants to Berkeley Law prohibits us from granting personal interviews.*
>
> *—Berkeley Law School*[1]

---

1 "FAQs," University of California Berkeley School of Law website, accessed April 2012, www.law.berkeley.edu/47.htm.

The overwhelming number of requests makes it logistically impossible for personal interviews to be offered as part of the admissions process.

—University of Virginia (UVA) Law School[2]

Regrettably, because of the high volume of applicants from all over the [United States] and abroad, it is not logistically possible for personal interviews to be included as part of the selection process.

—Columbia Law School[3]

While Berkeley, Columbia, and UVA note resource constraints, the University of Michigan's Law School does not elect to interview applicants for a variety of other reasons, including a lack of faith in the benefits of interviewing and concerns about the biases that interviews can create, and possibly also because of a history of legal battles related to affirmative action:[4]

We choose not to interview because social science research suggests that interviews offer no information helpful to the decision-making process; further, anecdotal evidence suggests that many fantastic and talented people do not always make a great first impression, particularly if the meeting takes place under the stressful circumstances of an evaluative interview. Interviews also present opportunities for discrimination on the basis of academically irrelevant personal characteristics, which we would prefer to avoid.

—University of Michigan Law School[5]

---

2 "Frequently Asked Questions–J.D. Admissions," University of Virginia School of Law website, accessed April 2012, www.law.virginia.edu/html/prospectives/faqs.htm.

3 "Application Review FAQ," Columbia Law School website, accessed April 2012, http://web.law.columbia.edu/admissions/jd/apply/faq/review.

4 In the 2003 case "Grutter vs. Bollinger," a Michigan Law School applicant who had been denied entry despite very competitive GPA and LSAT scores challenged the school's affirmative action policies, ultimately taking the issue to the U.S. Supreme Court. The court ultimately sided with the school, but Michigan legislators passed Proposal 2 soon after, which precluded the use of race in the admissions process.

5 "Frequently Asked Questions," University of Michigan Law School website, accessed April 2012, www.law.umich.edu/prospectivestudents/admissions/pages/faq.aspx.

Some other schools do not explain why they choose not to interview but do not mince words about their stance:

> *The Admissions Committee does not grant interviews as part of the admissions process.*

> *—Stanford Law School[6]*

> *We do not offer evaluative interviews and/or meetings with members of the Admissions Committee during the application process.*

> *—The University of Pennsylvania Law School[7]*

> *While the Committee on Admissions does not use interviews as part of the selection process, we would like to give you the opportunity to include more information about yourself than the application form conveys. Because people and their interests vary, we leave the content and length of your statement to your discretion.*

> *—New York University School of Law[8]*

Our primary piece of advice regarding schools that show or state no interest in interviewing candidates is that you should simply accept and observe their policies. Although you may want to believe differently, of course, you are not going to beat their door down and earn that special interview (just for you!) with a member of the admissions office. Repeatedly calling the school and requesting a meeting is a strategy that may work in the movies, but it is not a smart idea in reality. Put your energy and enthusiasm into your application instead, and then relax and wait to find out whether or not you got in. Simple as that.

---

6 "JD Application Procedure," Stanford Law School website, accessed April 2012, www.law.stanford.edu/program/degrees/jd/jd_application/.

7 "JD Admissions FAQ," The University of Pennsylvania Law School website, accessed April 2012, http://www.law.upenn.edu/prospective/jd/faq.html.

8 "Admissions Information and Instructions," New York University School of Law website, accessed April 2012, http://www.law.nyu.edu/admissions/jdadmissions/applicants/admissionsinformationandinstructions/index.htm.

INVITATION-ONLY INTERVIEWS

Some schools take a somewhat proactive approach toward interviews but certainly stop short of throwing open the floodgates. We see this spirit as "Don't call us. We'll call you ... *if* we want to learn more." Certain schools will not give *you* the option of scheduling an interview—possibly because allowing candidates this option would overwhelm the school with requests—but if your application piques their interest or gives rise to an unanswered question or two, they may reach out to you for an interview, in an effort to complete their total picture of you as an applicant:

We do not conduct personal interviews of all applicants and the Committee will not grant requests for interviews. Occasionally, the Admissions Committee will request an interview from an applicant if the Committee determines it would be helpful to the evaluation of the applicant's file.

—University of Chicago Law School[9]

Sometimes the Admissions Committee will request an evaluative interview. Due to our workload, we are not in a position to grant interviews upon applicant request.

—Cornell Law School[10]

When the admissions committee determines that additional information would be helpful in making a final decision, applicants may be invited to visit campus for an interview. These interviews are optional, and offered by invitation at the discretion of the admissions committee.

—Duke University School of Law[11]

---

9 "FAQs: How to Apply," University of Chicago Law School website, accessed April 2012, www.law.uchicago.edu/prospectives/jdfaq/howtoapply.

10 "Admission and Preparation," Cornell Law School website, accessed April 2012, www.lawschool.cornell.edu/admissions/FAQ/admission_and_preparation.cfm.

11 "Frequently Asked Questions," Duke University School of Law website, accessed April 2012, www.law.duke.edu/admis/faq.

Schools with this kind of approach to interviewing leave themselves the option in case they need to clarify certain points in your application or wish to evaluate some aspect of your personality or profile in a way that a paper or electronic application cannot sufficiently allow. Let us reassure you that if you apply to a law school with an interview policy like this and you do not receive an invitation to interview, you should not worry. No news is frequently good news for these schools. Again, definitely refrain from calling the admissions office and asking about or for an interview—this will only reflect on you negatively.

AS-NEEDED INTERVIEWS

The third most common approach to interviews is one we tend to interpret as "We intend to interview as many people as we can, but we won't necessarily interview you." Consider the following interview statements by two top law schools:

An alumni interview offers the Office of Admissions an opportunity to learn more about candidates beyond the written application. Those invited to interview are applicants the Admissions Committee wishes to know more about before making a decision. Alumni interviews also offer a unique opportunity for candidates to learn about Georgetown Law in a personal and meaningful way.

–Georgetown University Law Center

Harvard Law School is somewhat unique in that our admissions process involves a short, evaluative phone interview.

–Harvard Law School

Harvard Law School (HLS) does not interview every applicant, but every candidate it admits will have first been interviewed. Basically, what this means is that the school's admissions committee will read an applicant's file, and if the applicant is considered an appealing or promising candidate, that person will be granted a brief interview, which will help determine whether he or she is ultimately accepted to the JD program. In fact, HLS's admissions team calls between 1,000 and 1,200 candidates each year to yield the school's class of approximately 560 students.

Meanwhile, Georgetown has been growing its alumni interview program since 2007. The school is trying to interview more and more applicants, but interestingly, it does not *require* applicants to interview—in other words, a candidate can still be accepted to the school's JD program without first being interviewed. Applicants have the option of interviewing and will not be penalized if they choose not to do so.[12] Still, we suspect that few candidates would turn down such an opportunity to market themselves to the school. Among the country's top law schools, Georgetown and HLS are the only ones who will interview large numbers of applicants on a "get to know you" basis rather than to glean some specific clarification or information.

OPEN INTERVIEWS

In this fourth most popular interview approach, we imagine the law school telling applicants, "Our door is open. Come on in. We'd like to get to know you." But does any top law school really interview anyone and everyone who applies? Yes, in fact. Northwestern Law does—or, at least, is willing to do so— proudly describing itself on its website as "the only law school in the country that strongly encourages all applicants to interview as a part of the admissions process." The school's proactive approach allows it to keep an open mind about candidates and potentially discover the intangibles that will help it select the right ones from a competitive pool to foster a collegial community with the "cooperative culture for which [it is] known."

Northwestern is so serious about interviewing as many of its law school applicants as it can (and who want to be interviewed) that it has assembled a

---

12 "Alumni Admissions Interview Program," Georgetown Law website, accessed March 2012, www.law.georgetown. edu/admissions/AdmissionsInterviewProgram.htm.

veritable army of 700 alumni interviewers—yes, *700!*—in different cities, and it also makes staff members and students available to conduct interviews in the Chicago area. Candidates need not worry that they will be at a disadvantage if they interview with an alumnus or alumna rather than an admissions officer. Clearly, the school would not assemble a team of 700 if it was not going to take all its interview reports seriously.

§ The Purpose of the Interview

The schools that do interview, whether by invitation or by throwing the doors open to anyone who is interested, have many reasons for doing so. Some primary reasons include gauging your maturity, ensuring that you have the communication skills to succeed, learning more about your character by gathering more information about your interests and passions, confirming that you truly "get" law school and you have carefully considered their law school in particular, confirming that you have the necessary academic abilities, and creating a stronger connection between you and the school.

To Gauge Your Maturity

Acting in a mature manner for half an hour or less might sound easy to you, but this is probably because you are a legitimately mature person who does not need to fake it. However, some young law school applicants—many of whom attempt to go straight to law school from undergrad—may simply not be ready, even if they *think* they are, to manage the stresses inherent in law school, regardless of their life experience. Law schools want to be sure that the candidates they are considering have the maturity to navigate a very rigorous first-year curriculum and will ultimately be prepared to stand in front of other lawyers and earn that associate position. In short, they want people who are up for the challenges ahead and who will make them look good.

So, admissions officers may schedule a quick phone call or meeting with you as a way of gauging your true level of maturity, based typically on your confidence level, personal strengths, and even your reason for wanting to attend law school, which you may need to articulate to reveal that you have made a career choice. By having a conversation with you, your interviewer will be able to get a sense of the personality behind your application and truly understand that everything is indeed in place—that you are truly ready to handle the demands of law school.

TO ASSESS YOUR COMMUNICATION SKILLS

One of the stereotypes about lawyers is that they are great with books, but not so great with human beings. If your target school has gained a sense—via your recommendations or by reading between the lines in your life experiences—that you are academically savvy but not great at engaging others, they may want to speak with you directly to better evaluate your interpersonal skills. Again, your law school needs you to land a good job come graduation time, but they also want you to fit in well with your classmates while you are in the process of earning your JD. After a half hour or less with you on the phone or in person, someone should be able to assess how you interact with others and express yourself.

TO LEARN MORE ABOUT YOUR CHARACTER

Law schools are not interested in enrolling students who have great academic records or work histories but who have no personality or are completely one-dimensional. Your character is an important element of your overall profile—one that is not always easily or adequately communicated in an application—and schools want to admit candidates who can bring enthusiasm and "something unique" to their JD community. Moreover, schools often brag about the diversity of each class once the admissions season is over: "We have a former matador, an underwater welder, and a back-up singer for Justin Timberlake!"

Although some aspects of your personality can be conveyed in your essays, of course, the best way for an admissions officer to really understand what makes you tick can be to communicate with you directly—via an interview. Reading on paper that you are an avid scuba diver, for example, is informative, but to truly grasp your level of passion for and dedication to the sport, the interviewer might need to witness your speech patterns, word choice, and other such elements as you discuss your favorite pastime. In addition, he or she could collect more detail about your experiences via a direct conversation with you than you might be able to work into your application. You do not need to be wild, wacky, or intentionally unusual, but if you have a story to tell, your target law school likely wants to hear it!

TO ENSURE YOU KNOW WHAT TO EXPECT

Some law schools may wish to speak with you to determine not only whether you are truly ready for the rigors of the program, but also that you know how a JD will help you achieve your goals and that you have clear, specific reasons for wanting to attend law school. If you cannot offer any more detailed or thought-out response to "Why do you want to go to law school?" than "I am seeking a great general education," "I am a great debater and look forward to getting in front of the judge," or "I was inspired by *Boston Legal* and *The Practice*," you probably have not given law school enough thought, and this will, of course, not go over well with your interviewer. The admissions officers want to know that your decision to attend law school is not one you came to on a whim and is not some kind of default option for you, but that it is an academic and career choice that you have thoughtfully undertaken.

An interview also allows the school to better determine whether you have given proper, careful consideration to why you want to attend their program in particular. No admissions committee wants to extend an offer to an applicant who does not truly want to enroll in the school and will subsequently refuse the offer. So, if an admissions officer thinks you may be a good fit for the school but is unsure whether you are committed to enrolling should you be admitted, they may ask to interview you to better gauge—by engaging with you directly—your seriousness about their program. If you cannot explain, using specific examples and reasoned arguments, why you want (or even need) to earn your JD at *their* school, this will certainly not help your chances of being admitted. If you are invited to interview at your target program, be sure to prepare a thoughtful and detailed answer to send the right message.

To Confirm Your Academic Abilities

If you are borderline with respect to your LSAT score or your GPA compared with the averages for students at your target program, the school may want to do a little digging to learn more about you and your academic abilities. Maybe questions linger about inconsistencies on your transcript. Maybe your GPA or *one* of your LSAT scores leaves a lot to be desired, but everything else in your profile suggests that you would be a success in the JD program. In an interview, the admissions representative can delve further into the story behind these uncharacteristic data points to determine how important, if at all, these aberrations on your record might be. Your target school may need this small bit of reassurance to confirm that you have the skills necessary to do well in its JD program.

To Forge a Connection

Undoubtedly, all interviews involve a very subtle marketing component that flows from the school to the applicant. This is especially true for schools such as Northwestern Law and Georgetown Law, whose alumni—who obviously have a direct personal connection to the law school—engage significantly with candidates. Interviewing with a school essentially puts a human face (or voice) to it and, in the end, may make you *like* that school more than one with which you did not interview. If a program is interested in you as a candidate but suspects or knows that you may not be fully committed to it, the admissions committee may use an interview as a way of strengthening that connection.

§ How to Prepare for Your Interview

Although we do not recommend that you try to predict what will happen in your interview and choreograph responses to everything you expect to encounter, there *are* ways of preparing yourself for this important meeting that will increase your chances of having an effective and satisfying interview experience.

Have a Plan for Your Career

First, know what you want to do with your career and be ready to discuss it! The schools want to weed out any candidates who are applying to law school simply because they are being pressured to do so by overzealous parents or who just do not know what to do with themselves after graduating from college or reaching a lull or roadblock in their career. Not surprisingly, you will have a tough time expressing goals that you do not actually possess, and we can assure you that your admissions interviewer will quickly recognize when you are bluffing. Your interviewer is not going to try to evaluate whether you would ultimately be successful in the career to which you say you aspire; he or she simply wants to know that you have thought through your goals and have a plan in mind.

Explain Your School Choice

Second, know—and be able to intelligently articulate—why you want to go to the particular law school with which you are interviewing. Referring to the school's positive reputation or noting that a certain alumnus/alumna you admire attended the school is not sufficient. You will need to clearly demonstrate that you are familiar with the school's resources, not only by mentioning specific offerings in your answers, but also by explaining how these selected resources align with your unique needs and interests while in law school. You do not, however, need to try to "break new ground," so to speak, or to identify options with which the admissions officer him- or herself is unfamiliar, but you do need to speak about the program in a way that definitively proves that you have done your homework and have legitimate reasons for targeting that specific school. Avoid simply listing a number of centers, classes, and programs, and instead be sure you are ready to offer a reasoned and thoughtful discussion of the resources you intend to actually use. Consider the following sample responses to a typical "Why our school?" interview question:

Weak: *XYZ Law is a real leader in intellectual property law, and I am interested in this field. You have the professors, journals, speakers, and connections to make my post-law school dreams come true.*

Strong: *Given that I hope to become an intellectual property lawyer, I am particularly attracted to XYZ Law because of the school's program in intellectual property. I spoke with Dave Johnson from the Intellectual Property and Cyberlaw Society and learned about the "hot topics" symposia. When I checked out the roster of speakers, I was impressed by the variety of issues that were being discussed—everything from biotech patents to anti-counterfeiting—and I imagine such a breadth of exposure will prove invaluable to me in my career.*

Presumably, you have identified characteristics of and offerings at your target law program that appeal to you and that led you to apply to the school in the first place, in which case, you simply need to share this information with your interviewer in an honest and direct fashion. Very simply, if you believe it, the school—via your interviewer—will also believe it.

KNOW YOUR STORY

Third, be sure to know your own history cold. This step should be easy enough, because it is all about you! All you really have to do to prepare is review your résumé, reread your personal statement (and any other essays or addenda you may have submitted), and mentally go over your life in general, your reasons for applying to law school, and why you have specifically chosen to apply to the school with which you are interviewing. The admissions interviewer will not try to quiz you or ask you your opinion about news topics or historic Supreme Court judgments. Again, you will really only face questions that are about *you*.

In particular, take time to focus on your résumé and be ready to talk about the various accomplishments and activities you mentioned in it. For example, if you listed "French cinema" as an interest, be prepared to speak about a movie in this genre that you have recently seen. If you included the title of your undergrad thesis, be prepared to explain how you identified your thesis topic and perhaps how you performed the necessary research. In short, your interviewer may draw from your résumé or application for topics to discuss, so be sure you are ready to comment on any information you provided within it.

Moreover, be reassured that the question "What are your passions?" has no one "right" answer. You do not need to proclaim some fake and possibly absurd passion for your interviewer to see you as a sophisticated person—and if you were to do so, you could very well come across as just the opposite! To impress upon your interviewer that you are a genuine person, do not try to fudge or embellish your interests, just tell him or her what you are in fact passionate about.

THINK ANECDOTALLY

Fourth, think and prepare to speak anecdotally. As you look over your application in advance of your interview and review your major accomplishments, think about how you do things and come up with specific examples as illustrations. To revisit the "French cinema" example we mentioned in the previous section, you should not only be prepared to name a particular movie, but you should also be ready to tell a story related to it. The key to successfully answering an open-ended question like "What are your passions?" is to give examples that paint a picture of *how* you do what you do. You cannot merely say, "I am interested in film, sports, and cooking!" You need to expand on your answer and tell the story of and behind that interest. Consider the following example:

> *I have long had an interest in film and minored in film in college, where I not only took a few memorable classes in international cinema, but I also got to direct a five-minute short with a crew of five students, which was a real thrill. Today, I wish I had more time to keep up with the latest releases. Every once in a while, I can wrap up my day at the office early, and when that happens, I head to the theatre that is just a few blocks from my house and catch the late show. Sometimes I don't even know what they are showing. I just go and try my luck!*

You will notice that this individual's anecdote did not revolve around his winning the Palm d'Or at Cannes. You do not need to reveal something earth shattering to make an impression. This anecdote simply demonstrates the candidate's passion for film, which in turn reveals the candidate to be a passionate person. Take the time to think about *stories* that illustrate your accomplishments, experiences, and interests, and then practice responding to questions by using them thoughtfully.

PRACTICE

Perhaps you have heard the old joke, commonly (but possibly erroneously) attributed to violinist Jascha Heifetz, about the tourist in Manhattan who stopped the musician on the street to ask, "How do you get to Carnegie Hall?" To which Heifetz allegedly responded, "Practice." A less well-known but equally applicable quip is another one attributed to Heifetz: "If I don't practice one day, I know it; two days, the critics know it; three days, the public knows it." In other words, practice is key to success, including in your law school admissions interview. If you do not put in the work, to paraphrase Heifetz, "You will know it; your admissions interviewer will know it; your parents and friends will know it when they find out you did not get in."

Review the following questions, keeping in mind that you will not be asked all of them and that this list cannot possibly be exhaustive. Think about the stories you can use to illustrate your responses and then practice them:

Background Questions/Prompts

1. What decisions have you made that have brought you to this point—that have led you to apply to law school?

2. Who are you?

3. Tell me about yourself.

4. Walk me through your résumé.

5. How did you choose your college and major, and how did that lead you to the law, if at all?

Law School/The Law

1. Why do you want to be a lawyer?

2. What do you want to do with your law degree?

3. Where do you see a law degree taking you?

4. What would you like to learn in law school?

5. How did you decide that law school is for you?

6. Why do you want to attend our law school?

7. What sets our law school apart from others?

Leadership/Team Persona

1. Define your leadership style.

2. What role do you take on a team?

3. How do you approach team-oriented tasks?

4. Describe a challenging team interaction that you faced.

5. Tell me about an obstacle you have overcome. What did you learn about yourself?

6. Tell me about a time when you succeeded in a leadership position.

7. Tell me about a time when you failed in a leadership position.

8. How do you define success?

Personal

1. What do you do for fun?

2. What are your hobbies and passions?

3. What do you do outside work? Why?

4. Tell me about something you have done that people would not expect about you.

5. Tell me about a person who was an important influence on you.

6. What would your friends say about you?

Closing

1. Do you have any questions for me?

2. Is there anything else you would like me to know?

We strongly advise that in preparing for your interview, you sit in front of a mirror with a stopwatch to get a sense of your body language and to time your answers. You do not need to rehearse your answers to the exact second, but being ready to respond in a clear, focused, and concise way is important. For most questions, you should be able to answer in three minutes or less. If you take six or seven minutes to respond, you are likely rambling, may be using up time in which you could have offered the interviewer other important information about yourself, and will likely be boring your interviewer.

Whatever you do, do not attempt to memorize your answers. For one reason, you will likely end up sounding robotic rather than natural. For another, you will not be prepared if your interviewer should ask you a question that varies from the version for which you rehearsed. For example, if you memorize a specific response to the question "Why law school?" but the admissions representative instead asks you, "What would you like to learn in law school?," you might suddenly find yourself flailing—adding stress to an already challenging situation and no doubt botching a question you would otherwise be comfortable answering. Not only can you not predict what questions you will encounter in an interview and memorize perfect responses to each of them, but you also cannot anticipate and prepare for every possible permutation of every question. You are much better off simply *thinking about* your general responses and practicing more improvised answers.

DRESS FOR SUCCESS

If you are meeting your interviewer in person (as you will if you interview with Northwestern), you definitely need to dress appropriately. Doing so both serves as a sign of respect—for yourself, as well as for the school and the admissions representative—and says something about your maturity. This is not the time to try scoring points for individuality by showing up in jeans and a T-shirt. Showing some creativity and style with your clothing is okay, but do not go overboard—remember that your meeting is essentially a professional one, and you want to make a good impression. You can contact your target law school's admissions office to inquire about appropriate interview attire, but we recommend that you always consider business attire your default, even at law school forums. If you expect to interact with admissions officers, you should make the effort to put your best foot forward.

PREPARE MEANINGFUL QUESTIONS

As you can see from our list of closing questions presented a few sections earlier, for an interviewer to finish an interview by asking, "Do you have any questions about our school?" is not uncommon. When responding, you would be well advised to reveal that you have done your homework on the school. The interview is not the time for you to learn about the school, but rather an opportunity to ask insightful questions that inferentially showcase your knowledge of the school or that indicate that you are critically evaluating your options. For example, this is not the time to ask, "Do you have any classes in environmental law?" If you were truly interested in environmental law, you would already know the answer to this question. However, you could say, for example, "I was impressed to see that you recently hired two new environmental law professors. Was this part of a strategy to grow in this area?" Such a question shows that you are aware of what is taking place on campus and are evaluating the school in part based on this change—you have not just considered the school's ranking or reputation and decided to apply, but have really done your research and weighed your options.

Avoid overarching exploratory questions ("What should I know about your constitutional law offerings?") and vague questions with no direct connection to your goals ("What do *you* like about the law school?"), while also keeping in mind who your interviewer is—alumni may not know specifics about recent changes to curriculum, for example, whereas admissions personnel may not have as much insight into workplace issues (as an alumnus or alumna would). Your goal in asking questions is to show that you are an intelligent consumer of law school education, carefully doing your research and making informed choices. You want to send the message that you know what you are getting into and that you are applying for a reason—a message the admissions committee will find quite appealing.

§ CONCLUSION

Overwhelmingly, law school interviews are not intended to trip you up, expose your weaknesses, and exclude you from consideration for admission. On the contrary, they are opportunities for the school to gain further insight into who you are and for you to reveal your personality and help your admissions interviewer better understand your character. Rather than stressing about your interview, try to get in the mind-set of "this is an opportunity" and have fun with the experience. Excuse the cliché, but if you relax and focus on being yourself, you should have a very positive interview experience.

CHAPTER 7

WHAT HAPPENS IN LAW SCHOOL?

Congratulations! You aced the LSAT, wrote a profound and compelling personal statement, earned the praise of your recommenders, and were a stellar student to start, so you were not surprisingly accepted to the law school of your choice. But after you finish celebrating, you may start to wonder what exactly you can expect to encounter when you arrive to begin your studies. Will the experience feel like a few bonus years of college, or will you be engaged in a three-year battle of "all work and no play"? Although each person's experience will vary, law school can be an academically rigorous, personally fulfilling, and, yes, even fun experience. So, before you head off to campus and officially become a 1L (first-year law student), read on to learn some basics of what law school is really like.

§ An Introduction to Academics

Let us start with an examination of what the classroom experience will be like. You may be surprised to learn that your law school education will begin even before you set foot on campus, because you will likely have a substantial amount of reading to do. Yes, you read that correctly: you will have homework *before* the first day of school. Students must cover so much material in law school that professors tend to dive right into substantive material. So, sometime during the summer before your first year, your professors will probably contact you with your first assignment. Typically, this will involve approximately 30 pages of fairly dense reading for each class. In law school, however, you will not be using traditional textbooks; instead, you will need to get used to working with **casebooks**, which are large (and often quite expensive) tomes filled with legal cases that address the particular area of law being studied in each course. Usually authored by well-known professors, casebooks do not simply outline the various principles of law, but instead present representative cases that allow students to analyze the legal doctrine themselves.

The casebook method was developed in 1890 by Christopher Columbus Langdell, the then-dean of Harvard Law School, and was quickly adopted by nearly all law schools. Rather than involving rote lectures on **blackletter law**—the term used to refer to basic principles of law that are accepted by a majority of judges in most states—classes are based on the reading and analysis of actual legal cases, which allows students to become familiar with the principles that underlie the law and their application in practice. As a result, as a law school student, you will learn more about legal theory than about the letter of the law. Some people debate the merits of this system, with detractors arguing that students ultimately graduate from law school unprepared to actually be lawyers. However, the casebook method continues to be popular because it teaches students to think critically about the law and to apply rules to different fact patterns.

In the long run, the skills you will gain via the casebook method will likely serve you better in your legal practice than would the rote memorization of the law. Clients do not want to pay big bucks for a lawyer to just rattle off something they could learn themselves via a quick Google search; they want a trained legal specialist who can help them get the outcome they want. Reading cases will teach you to learn to think abstractly and flexibly about the law, so you can be that desirable "legal mind."

So, you now have a grasp of what casebooks are and are ready to purchase the ones you need, but which classes will you be taking? Perhaps surprisingly, many law schools have similar curricula. No matter which JD program you attend, in your first year, you will most likely take some version of the following courses: "Torts," "Contracts," "Civil Procedure," "Criminal Law," and "Property." This base curriculum was also pioneered at Harvard Law School by Langdell and quickly became the standard at law schools across the country—as it remains today. The class "Constitutional Law" was not a part of Langdell's original formulation, but it is also commonly taught as a core curriculum course, as is the nearly ubiquitous legal research and writing course that goes by different names at different schools, but covers similar material. The following is a short guide to the standard 1L schedule:

"Civil Procedure" ("Civ Pro"): This course is an overview of the rules that govern civil justice procedures. For example, you will learn the rules for filing motions, how to have the proper jurisdiction to try a case, and how civil trial proceedings work. Some students may find this course a little dry, but it is also one of the most useful first-year courses, because you will likely encounter the rules it teaches early in your legal career.

"Constitutional Law" ("Con Law"): In this course, you will study in great detail the famous Supreme Court cases that may sound familiar from your high school American History classes. (*Marbury v. Madison*, anyone?) You will learn about the role of the courts in our government's system of checks and balances and will likely engage in some interesting debates about hot-button issues such as gay rights and abortion. In this class, you will learn the most from your classmates if you can keep an open mind.

"Contracts": This class—another one that will likely prove useful early in your career—covers the elements of what makes an agreement binding, as well as what happens when someone breaches such an agreement. You will study many old, established court cases but will also cover the Uniform Commercial Code. You will probably find this course useful in your day-to-day life as well, as you sign leases, put your John Hancock on an employment agreement, or say yes to "click-through" software licenses.

"Criminal Law" ("Crim"): A favorite class of many 1Ls, this one covers the stuff that shows like *Law & Order* are made of: murder, rape, robbery. You will learn the elements that constitute these kinds of crimes, as well as the defenses and justifications used to excuse them, and will no doubt have some stimulating discussions about the morality of the American criminal justice system.

"Property": This class focuses on the concept of how things are owned. You will learn the incredibly complex rules of possessing both personal property and real property (i.e., land). If you think the answer is as simple as "finders keepers," you will discover that you have a lot to learn in this course, which is riddled with such strange concepts as "the fertile octogenarian" (we will let you look that one up on your own). You may initially forget much of what you learn in this class after the final, but be warned, it will show up on the bar exam three years later.

"Torts": **Tort** is the term for a legal wrong, and in this class, you will read cases about the obligations individuals have to others that are imposed by law (rather than by contracted agreement). For example, you have a legal duty to not drive drunk. If you drive drunk, criminal charges can of course be brought against you, but if your drunk driving causes harm to another person, you may also be responsible for paying that person (or his or her estate) a sum of money to compensate for the injuries sustained. The concept of tort reform, or capping the amount of money a person or organization can be ordered to pay, is a hotly debated issue right now, so make sure to pay attention in class!

"First-Year Writing and Research": This is arguably the most important class you will take in your first year. In this course, you will learn the elements of drafting those all-important legal documents: the **memo** and the **brief**. As a new attorney, you will spend a substantial amount of your time researching, writing, and editing memorandums (memos) of law, which are objective analyses of legal issues and are often presented to partners and clients to provide background on relevant issues. And if you become a litigator, as many of you will, you will become extremely familiar with briefs. A legal brief is a persuasive document presented to a court that argues why your side is correct and should prevail.

This class also teaches research skills and how to use online legal databases such as LexisNexis and Westlaw. Whatever field of law you enter, legal research will likely make up the bulk of what you do, and time will be of the essence. This course teaches you tricks and tips to researching quickly and efficiently.

In 2006, Harvard Law School made some significant changes to its 1L course load—the first major overhaul of the first-year curriculum since the adoption of Langdell's original formulation. Then-dean Elena Kagan (now a Supreme Court Justice) said of the changes, "Over 100 years ago, Harvard Law School invented the basic law school curriculum, and we are now making the most significant revisions to it since that time."[1] The new course requirements add three classes to the first-year curriculum: a course on legislation and regulation, a choice of courses introducing global legal issues, and a course that focuses on problem solving. The philosophy behind the new curriculum is to better prepare students for the actual practice of law, to incorporate international aspects of the law, and to recognize that regulations and statutes are as vital to the law as court decisions are. Other JD programs, including the Emory University School of Law and the College of Law at Michigan State University, have made similar adjustments to adapt to the changing field of law. However, Langdell's original core curriculum continues to be the standard at most law schools.

---

1   Elaine McArdle, "A Curriculum of New Realities: At Harvard Law School, some new answers to the question, What do future lawyers need to know?" *Harvard Law Bulletin*, Winter 2008. www.law.harvard.edu/news/bulletin/2008/winter/feature_1.php.

§ Life in the JD Classroom

You now have all your casebooks, you have completed your first readings, and you are sitting in your very first law school class with your laptop open, ready to start taking notes (however you did it as an undergraduate, in law school, you will use a computer to take notes in class). Take a moment to look around, because you are going to get to know these particular fellow students very well in the coming months: they are your section mates. Most law schools split their incoming 1L classes into smaller **sections** of anywhere from 30–80 people, depending on the size of the school, and you will take all of your first-year classes with this set group of people.

Some of these classmates will impress you, some will intimidate you, some will become your best friends, and some will, unfortunately, get on your nerves. Regardless of how you feel about each classmate, staying on good terms with as many of them as possible is in your best interest. Because you will be consuming so much information, you should be prepared to set aside any competitiveness to work together—and this means lending others your notes when asked, knowing that you will need to borrow someone else's at some point. In the end, you will all be graded on your own individual merit, based on your performance on just one, blind-graded final exam, so when your section mate is cold-called and sends you an SOS instant message, do not leave him or her hanging, because you might need that favor returned one day. Not sure what cold-calling is? A cornerstone of the Socratic method, **cold-calling** is when a professor selects a student at random to begin the day's classroom discussion of the topic at hand. Let us turn our focus, then, to what happens when the professor begins class.

The Old Standard: The Socratic Method

When you imagine a law school classroom, the first image that comes to your mind is likely that of a ruthless professor mercilessly interrogating a terrified student about the minutest nuances of the law. If so, what you are picturing is an exaggerated version of the **Socratic method** in action. In this teaching approach—named, as you may have guessed, for the Greek philosopher Socrates—the professor asks students question after question to stimulate critical thinking, explore the depths of the students' knowledge, and push the boundaries of their capabilities. Rather than simply lecturing on a topic while students take notes, the professor will call on a student at random—in other words, "cold-call" a student—and continue to question that student until he or she simply runs out of answers. This teaching method has always been used in law schools and remains the predominate method today.

Although being in the Socratic hot seat can be intimidating, many students find these kinds of classes exciting and appealing. Students in courses taught this way are generally well prepared, and class conversations can be extremely engaging. Moreover, law is a field in which you will often be put on the spot, whether by opposing counsel in court, your client on a conference call, or a partner in a meeting, so learning to think on your feet and remain cool in high-pressure situations is vital to your success—and is one of the most important skills you can gain in law school. And fortunately, most law school professors today are kinder and more forgiving than the stereotypical ones you have seen in the movies. Still, keeping your head when the spotlight is on you can be tough, so here are some tips to help you manage the Socratic method:

1. **Be prepared.** You may have aced college without ever cracking the binding on your books, but that will not fly in law school. Even the quickest thinker will be thrown off by the often tricky trajectory of Socratic questioning if he or she is not adequately familiar with the material. If you want to be sure to succeed when the professor calls your name, always read the assigned cases carefully, think through them thoroughly, and perhaps discuss your thoughts with a friend or two before class. Some people like to take notes on cases (this is known as **briefing** a case), some prefer to work with other students in study groups, some purchase commercially prepared course outlines that cover the most common law school cases, and others simply do a very

close reading on their own. Some students even do all four. Briefing cases tends to be very common among first-semester 1Ls, though this activity usually tapers off entirely by 2L year. Find the process that works best for you and use your time efficiently.

2. **If you are *not* prepared, tell the professor.** It will happen. Whatever the reason—from illness to other work to social engagements—the bottom line is that come class time, if you are not prepared, the professional thing to do is inform the professor before class. Having an awkward exchange with the professor in the middle of class is not in anyone's best interests. Many professors will allow students a certain number of "passes" per semester, and we know of at least one Harvard Law School professor who requires students to file a "notice of unpreparedness" in advance of class. Your professors are human, too, and they understand that things come up. Show them respect by owning up to your unpreparedness (and keeping such instances to a minimum), and they will return that respect.

3. **Do not dwell on a screw-up.** Nearly every former law student we know can recall at least one time (and usually more) when they did not exactly shine in class during Socratic questioning. We assume that if you are the kind of person who aspires to law school, you are likely accustomed to succeeding and have trouble forgetting those times when you made a somewhat public mistake. The good news is that no one else will remember, so do not be overly concerned if your responses are less than stellar now and then. Keep in mind that you are there to learn, and you cannot expect to always have the right answer the first time. And perhaps more importantly, remember that law school grades are usually based entirely on your performance on the final exam, and because these tests are blind graded (more on this in the next section), your performance in class will never directly affect your GPA.

4. **Enjoy the ride.** One thing we can claim with some confidence is that you will never forget the thrill of being cold-called and answering a succession of questions correctly—and if you do the work, this *will* happen. The feeling that you are finally starting to master the complex material you are studying is really its own reward. And once you have survived your first Socratic experience unscathed, you can celebrate— you have survived a law school initiation right.

IT ALL COMES DOWN TO THIS: THE FINAL EXAM

Almost all law school classes are graded entirely on the student's performance on one final exam, which is blind-graded (yet another Langdell innovation). **Blind grading** means that the exam is graded without the student's name on it—an identification number is used instead—so that the professor's personal opinion of the student will not have any influence on the final grade. In Langdell's time, professors not uncommonly gave better grades to students of higher socioeconomic status. Langdell, who came from modest means, wanted to avoid this kind of bias, so he instituted the blind grading policy. This means that today, all those hours sweating over the Socratic method have little bearing on your final grade… well, kind of.

The best way to prepare yourself for your law school exams is to do the required work all semester long—if you try to cram for the exams at the end of the semester, you will make your life much more difficult than it needs to be. First, keep in mind that most law school exams are both open book and open note, so make sure that you are paying attention in class and taking careful notes. Do not let the concept of an open book test mislead you into thinking your exams will be easy. Law school exams rarely require straightforward fact recitation. On most, you will be given several stories of bizarre situations, known as **fact patterns**, and then asked to identify the legal issues involved, determine applicable laws and rules, and analyze the outcome of each issue.

The exams come in different formats. Some will be take-home tests, which you will generally have between 8 and 24 hours to complete. Alternatively, shorter exams (approximately three hours long) may be given in the classroom. Either way, you will be expected to do a lot of writing on these exams in a limited amount of time, and this is where meticulous note-taking will come in handy. Given that the bulk of what you will be writing is your individual analysis of the case presented, you will want to be able to access the applicable rules very quickly, so you will be able to devote the maximum amount of time possible to the substance of the test.

As we noted earlier, law students take notes on their laptops rather than in notebooks, and this makes converting mass quantities of notes into organized **outlines**—condensed versions of notes within which key information can be readily located—much easier. Commercial outlines are available, and you may also be able to obtain outlines from students from prior years, but creating your own outline is best, because it will be specifically tailored to your particular class and will be written in your own voice. You will probably be able to access your outline on your computer during the exam, and having this kind of easily searchable document at hand is immensely helpful. Approach law school exam preparation as a marathon rather than a sprint, and you will find yourself calm and collected on exam day—and more likely to be pleased when grades are released.

§ Beyond 1L: It Gets Better!

You may have heard the old adage about law school: "The first year they scare you to death, the second year they work you to death, and the third year they bore you to death." This saying is an oft repeated one, but it is not exactly true. First year, as we have discussed, is not necessarily all that frightening, and second and third year are full of fascinating experiences. Although some law schools do have a few required courses for advanced students—often some version of "Administrative Law," "Professional Responsibility," and/or "Evidence"—you will mostly take electives in your second and third years. Many students choose to take more traditional classes, such as "Corporations," "Taxation," and "Securities," and some make the mistake of trying to take courses they feel will best prepare them for the bar exam, but this is not necessary. Do not worry about the bar exam now—you will learn everything you need to know for the exam the summer before you take it. Instead, enjoy the academic experience of law school and follow your intellectual heart.

Another bonus of your 2L and 3L years is that some electives, known as **seminars**, are much smaller than standard classes (10–20 people rather than 30–80) and allow for a more interactive and deeper learning experience. Traditional classes definitely have their place in the curriculum and provide a useful foundation for actual practice, but more and more, law schools are trying to entice students with some sexier subjects. Here are a few unusual law school classes you might find intriguing:

- **"Animal Law"** (Fordham University School of Law): Focuses on laws related to animal laboratory testing, animal fighting, and animals used for entertainment or religious purposes.

- **"Children and the Law"** (University of Texas, Austin, School of Law): Discusses the laws designed to protect children living in a traditional family setting, what happens when the state intervenes in that setting, and the issues that arise when children are raised outside a setting that would constitute a family unit.

- **"Law and Creativity: Fiction and Nonfiction"** (Stanford Law School): Addresses the creative treatment of legal issues in film and literature; students submit and discuss their own creative writing.

- **"Amateur Sport Law"** (Marquette University Law School): Covers Title IX gender discrimination, the resolution of disputes affecting Olympic sports, and the regulation of private educational institutions and sports associations, and focuses on the legal regulation of interscholastic, intercollegiate, and Olympic sports.

- **"Motion Picture Distribution"** (University of California, Los Angeles, School of Law): Provides a small group of students with an introduction to the distribution of theatrical motion pictures, starting with exhibition in theaters and moving to home video, video on demand, and television; also considers new distribution technologies for motion pictures, including the Internet and mobile devices.

After the 1L year, the format of classes tends to move away from the Socratic method. Although many classes will still use this method, some professors will instead assign students to "panels"—telling students in advance which weeks they will be called on. In other classes, student participation will be completely voluntary. The additional flexibility this provides in your reading schedule will be welcome, because you will start to have more responsibilities outside the classroom.

CONNECT WITH THE COMMUNITY THROUGH CLINICS

During your 2L and 3L years, you will have the opportunity to step off campus and apply your skills in the real world. Many law schools offer **clinics**, in which students receive credit for representing real clients. That is right—you will get to actually practice law—though with supervision, of course. Clinics allow students to hone their practical lawyering skills—a big draw for prospective employers—while also serving the community. For example, students involved in the University of Washington School of Law's Race and Justice Clinic advocate for better treatment of youth of color in the juvenile justice, child welfare, and education systems. In the Duke University School of Law's Guantanamo Defense Clinic, students assist with the representation of defendants charged for trial at Guantanamo, preparing briefs, motions, and other filings for military commission and federal court proceedings. The Samuelson Law, Technology and Public Policy Clinic at Berkeley Law (University of California) gives students the chance to counsel both small and large clients on important issues related to law and technology, such as biotech, copyright, and patent reform. Though not a requirement, if you want to know what practicing law is really like, take advantage of the clinic opportunities offered at your school.

THE FINAL FRONTIER: THE 3L WRITING REQUIREMENT

You have survived three years of demanding coursework, have a job lined up for the fall, and the bar exam is still at least six weeks away, but one thing still stands between you and your diploma: the 3L writing requirement. Many law schools require students to write a law-related document of approximately 20–30 pages in length. The American Bar Association mandates that law students take at least one course as a 2L or 3L that requires the writing of a paper for credit, and a written paper requirement is an easy way for law schools to ensure that students meet this criterion. Schools tend to be fairly flexible with this requirement (for example, we know of people who have turned in law-themed screenplays and novellas—and gotten As), but make sure you know what is required at your school. And try not to leave this assignment until the last minute. After three years of hard work, you should be preparing to celebrate your graduation, not sweating over getting your last assignments done.

§ EXTRACURRICULAR ACTIVITIES

A well-rounded law school education involves more than attending classes. If you just fulfill your academic requirements, you will of course earn your diploma, but you will miss out on the greater benefits of being part of a community of ambitious, legally minded colleagues. To get the most from your JD experience, be sure to take advantage of the school's extracurricular resources that interest you, engage with some of the student organizations, and simply take some time away from your studies now and then.

JOIN A JOURNAL

Many people consider law journals the primary extracurricular activity at law school, and to an extent, this is true. A **law journal** is a student-edited publication of legal scholarship that typically includes full-length articles on timely legal topics—generally written by law professors, judges, or legal practitioners—and shorter pieces, such as notes, comments, essays, and book reviews—often written by the journal's student members. Journal members are generally referred to as editors. Student journal members can also hold executive board positions in some cases, and thereby have the opportunity to make business decisions related to the publication. Contributing to such a journal is a popular extracurricular activity choice in part because employers like to see a journal membership on résumés (particularly if the student in question has written a note or case comment). In addition, working as a journal editor helps improve many of the skills students will need in their law career, such as clean writing, attention to detail, and project management.

Not all law school journals are created equal, however. Most programs will have a journal called the Law Review, which is the school's most prestigious publication. A writing competition, which involves both writing and editing, is used to determine which students are selected as Law Review editors. However, most schools have a host of other journals as well, and contributing to one of these is typically much easier. These journals also tend to have a more specific focus. Some examples include the *Journal of Catholic Legal Studies* (St. John's University School of Law), the *Northwestern Journal of Technology and Intellectual Property* (Northwestern University School of Law), the *Law Journal for Social Justice* (Arizona State University's Sandra Day O'Connor College of Law), and the *Texas Hispanic Journal of Law & Policy* (University of Texas Law School).

Some schools will let students join these "secondary" journals as 1Ls, but most hold their writing/editing competitions the summer after the 1L year. If you want to work at a big law firm, joining a journal is not mandatory, but it is certainly a wise choice. If you aspire to hold a prestigious position with a federal judge (a **clerkship**), it is basically nonnegotiable, because judges rarely hire JDs who do not have any journal experience. Whether you should aim to secure a position on your school's Law Review or choose to contribute to a journal that focuses on your specific area of interest within the legal realm will depend largely on the size and reputation of the law school you attend. If your program is perhaps considered less illustrious, you would benefit from being a part of the best journal your school has to offer. This will reflect especially well on you when you are later conducting your job search.

MAKE YOUR MARK IN MOOT COURT

Moot Court is another popular law school activity with great appeal to employers. In the American court system, cases are heard first at what is known as the trial level, where evidence and testimony are initially presented. If the decision of the trial court requires review, the reviewable issues are brought on appeal to an appellate court. In Moot Court, selected students prepare simulated appellate-level cases and argue them in front of judges during national or international competitions. Judges are often law professors, local attorneys, and sometimes even practicing, real-world judges. Students typically spend a semester researching the assigned case and writing briefs in preparation for oral arguments. Judges ask impromptu questions throughout oral arguments, and students must be comfortable responding extemporaneously. In addition to honing their public speaking abilities, Moot Court members spend many hours perfecting their legal analytical, research, and writing skills, and these are skills employers want to see. Law schools have different processes for selecting Moot Court members, and membership can be quite competitive, especially at schools that are used to having successful teams at national competitions.

BEER TASTING AND BASKETBALL: STUDENT ORGANIZATIONS

Something that sets law schools apart from many other doctorate-level educational programs is the wide array of student activities and organizations they offer. Some of these are law related, of course, such as the Art Law Society at the Boston University School of Law, whereas others, such as the Board Game Enthusiasts at Georgetown Law, are just for fun and give students an occasional escape from their studies. Because law schools tend to be large enough to function as their own mini universities, they often have every type of student organization you would expect to find at an undergraduate program. For example, law schools have their own newspapers, a cappella groups, and student governments, and most will have student groups for various religious, ethnicities, cultures, pastimes, and political affiliations.

Through these activities you can take the edge off the stress that often goes hand in hand with the required workload—not to mention that involvement with student organizations can also help you stand out to future employers. During on-campus interviewing, law students who walk into an interview with nothing more to distinguish them from every other student than the standard journal membership and a 3.3 GPA will not make the same impression as a student who can discuss her experience as president of the Women's Law Association or one who is a member of the school's improvisational comedy troupe. Demonstrating your ability to do well academically while participating (or even excelling) in other activities at the same time will indicate to potential employers that you can multitask efficiently. And when you make the leap from law student to lawyer, maintaining a sense of work-life balance will be essential to your sanity, so work on practicing that skill while in school.

Five Nonscholarly Student Organizations You Can Join in Law School

1. **In Vino Veritas** (Harvard Law School): Members of this society develop their wine appreciation skills through tastings, receptions, and wine-paired dinners.

2. **The Emory Food Club** (Emory Law): Emory foodies band together to discover area restaurants and bars with fellow law students and other graduate students, and enjoy a temporary respite from their studies.

3. **Ete Bowl** (University of Hawaii Richardson School of Law): Female law school students participate in flag football, and play each year in the Ete Bowl, a game between current students and alumnae.

4. **Alpine Society** (Columbia Law School): This group organizes snowboarding, rock climbing, and hiking excursions for law students, and coordinates weekend and spring break trips to a variety of ski resorts.

5. **The Libel Show** (University of Virginia School of Law): Approximately 200 law students write, produce, and star in this annual theatrical production featuring song parodies and skits that take a lighthearted look at life at the law school.

SOCIAL LIFE: THE REWARDS OF HARD WORK

By now, you have probably grasped that fulfilling the course work and job search–related responsibilities of a law student will take up a lot of your time, but earning your JD does not have to be all work and no play. After all, law firms do not generally have sports teams (save the occasional summer softball league) or drama societies, so your law school years could represent your last major opportunity for a while to pursue these sorts of hobbies and spend some quality social time with friends. And do not restrict yourself to campus-based opportunities either. Yes, you are busy, but you are also in the rather rare position of having total control over how you spend most of your time.

Contrary to popular belief, perhaps, law schools do not expect students to spend every second immersed in their studies. Most schools host "Bar Reviews" on set weekday nights (typically Thursdays), when students go to a local bar to enjoy some drinks and unwind. And most JD programs offer special celebrations and parties throughout the academic experience. At the New York University School of Law, for example, students look forward to the annual Fall Ball costume party, Spring Fling musical theme night, and Barristers' Ball end-of-the-year celebration for 3Ls. The Gamma Eta Gamma Law House is a cooperative at the University of Minnesota Law School that hosts welcome parties for 1Ls, Halloween festivities, and barbecues. Harvard Law School's social website, hlcentral.com, presents a list of events that include formal dances, tailgates, and concerts. And keep your eyes open for law firm receptions, which are usually held at swanky restaurants and feature free food and cocktails (student budget friendly!). Finally, of course, you will make friends in law school, and together you will enjoy some great social experiences outside the classrooms and courtrooms.

§ THE JOB SEARCH

Learning for the sake of learning is a beautiful thing, but the point of attending law school is obviously to become a lawyer. After committing your time, energy, and money for three years to earn your JD, you will most definitely want to graduate with a job in hand. Law school graduates go on to fulfill many different roles, and we know some who have even taken positions outside the typical legal field, becoming professors, writers for Jimmy Kimmel, in-house counsel for such companies as Etsy.com and CBS, novelists, and PhD students. Law students find the more typical legal positions primarily through two specific job-search processes: Law Firm On-Campus Interviewing (OCI) and Clerkship Applications.

BigLaw and On-Campus Interviewing

Traditionally, most law students dreamed of landing a gig in BigLaw: that is, at one of the 1,000-lawyer mega firms that bill clients at rates of $750 an hour and pay even a first-year associate a solid six-figure salary. In the economy's heyday, these firms were giving summer positions to both 1Ls and 2Ls that paid $2,400 a week for the taxing "job" of eating five-course lunches at expensive restaurants and culminated in guaranteed offers of permanent employment post-graduation. We hate to be the bearer of bad news, but those days seem to be over, at least for the moment. The number of students who will be offered associate positions each year varies from school to school, of course, but one universal truth stands: if you want to be considered for one of these lucrative positions, you will have to take part in on-campus interviewing, better known as OCI.

During OCI, which takes place in the late summer or early fall, depending on the school, law firms will come to campus and take over classrooms and hotels. Although some firms will use OCI to interview 3Ls seeking full-time post-graduation jobs, and a separate, smaller OCI may sometimes be offered in the spring for 1Ls seeking a summer job at a firm, for the most part, OCI is an activity for 2Ls looking for summer internships (known as summer associateships) that they hope will later result in an offer for a permanent position. The activity requires a lot of work and can be quite stressful, and as a student at George Washington University Law School told us, "OCI puts the most pressure on students of anything and makes early 2Ls look back at their mediocre first year."

OCI can last from one week to three weeks, depending on the JD program, and competition for OCI interview slots likewise varies from school to school. At some schools, students have the option of meeting with any firm they can fit into their schedules. At most schools, though, the bid process is more selective: students must rank the firms at which they wish to interview and submit résumés to those firms; the firms then select which of those candidates they deem most promising and interview just the selected students. Desirable students at well-known schools can have five or more interviews in a single day and as many as 30 interviews total, though approximately ten interviews over the course of the OCI period is more standard.

In these 20-minute interviews, students of course do their best to wow the interviewing law firm partners with their personalities, though in reality, their chances of being invited to a second-round, or **callback**, interview are based largely on the quality of their transcripts and résumés. In this super-competitive world, give yourself every advantage. Make sure both you and your résumé look neat and professional, and take advantage of any workshops or mock interview opportunities your school's career services office provides. In addition, although firms can start to seem quite similar after a while, always take the time to diligently research each one individually before your interview. Familiarize yourself with the firm's practice areas and learn what makes each firm stand out. Not only do employers want to hear that you have taken special interest in their firm in particular, but you also do not want to find yourself talking about your passion for art law in an interview with a firm that does not have an art law practice. Doing your due diligence will pay dividends.

Should you be lucky enough to receive a callback interview offer, you will be invited to visit the office at the firm's expense; they will fly you in and put you up in a hotel, and will usually provide you with a nice meal or two as well. You will meet with approximately four attorneys for roughly 30 minutes each, usually a senior partner, a junior partner, a senior associate, and a junior associate. Quite often, two junior associates will take you out for lunch. Although this lunch is generally not evaluative and serves as a good opportunity for you to ask questions about the position and firm more informally, you will need to remember your table manners and continue to present yourself in a professional manner throughout.

If you are offered a summer associateship at a BigLaw firm, you may feel that you have hit the jackpot. These jobs tend to pay well—approximately $35,000 for the summer—and come with plenty of perks, such as nice meals and fun outings, even if these may be a bit sparser now than in years prior. However, unlike past summer associates, you will likely be expected to do a fair amount of work and, unfortunately, will not be guaranteed a permanent offer. So do not waste this golden opportunity if it is given to you—go into your summer expecting to do everything in your power to earn that offer.

FEDERAL CLERKSHIPS

An alternative, but equally prestigious, career path to working at a law firm is a federal judicial clerkship. A federal clerkship can be a great stepping stone to a plum government position, which can come with the potential for a six-figure salary and significant job security. Judicial law clerks work for judges and assist them with researching the legal issues brought before the judges. Clerks also help draft the judges' opinions, which are written reports of the reasoning behind the judges' various rulings. Law clerks can have significant influence on the legal determinations judges reach. For this reason, these clerkships tend to be highly selective; the judges want only the best and the brightest working for them and normally do not look much further than the very top of the class when making hiring decisions. Often, they will not even consider applications from candidates who do not have law journal experience (and some judges are only interested in candidates with Law Review experience). These clerkships are becoming increasingly more competitive, and some federal judges receive as many as a thousand applications for each available slot.

Several types of federal clerkships are available. The most prestigious of these is a position with a U.S. Supreme Court Justice; 36 of these positions—maximum—are available each year (four for each justice; although the chief justice has the option of having a fifth clerk, this is rarely exercised), and clerking with a judge on the federal court of appeals is a prerequisite to clerking on the Supreme Court. Therefore, a U.S. Court of Appeals clerkship is the next most prestigious and difficult position to obtain, particularly one with a judge who is known to be a "feeder" to the Supreme Court. Clerkships with U.S. District

Court judges are the next most competitive, and the popularity of the position varies by geographic location. Finally, federal clerkships are also available with lower-level trial court judges, United States Tax Court Special Trial judges, and bankruptcy judges, whose cases can be appealed to U.S. District Court. Ultimately, the choice of which clerkship(s) to pursue is up to you, but you may want to meet with an adviser from your law school to make sure you apply to an appropriate range of positions.

Working as a law clerk can open up many other subsequent career opportunities, ranging from positions at law firms to judicial appointments—in fact, six of our current Supreme Court justices were once clerks for previous justices! Firms like to hire former clerks, both because they can rest assured that these individuals have excellent writing and reasoning skills, and because they know the former clerks possess substantial practical experience. As a result, firms often offer large bonuses to associates who clerked before joining the firm.

Until recently, the process of obtaining a federal clerkship had been an extremely unwieldy one. Now, however, the introduction of the Online System for Clerkship Application and Review (known as OSCAR), a centralized resource that coordinates clerkship applications and the hiring system, has streamlined the process considerably. Nearly every federal judge permits candidates to apply via this system—and many actually require it—so for each judge for whom you wish to clerk, you can simply upload your cover letter, résumé, transcript, and letters of recommendation to OSCAR. Some judges do still require paper applications, however, and these must be sent via FedEx. Law schools will coordinate paper applications on your behalf; on a designated day, you bring the school all your applications and enough money to cover the shipping costs, and the school will send the files out for you.

For the most part, the National Federal Judges Law Clerk Hiring Plan dictates the dates when federal judges may receive applications from matriculating 3Ls, contact applicants, and interview and hire law clerks. First, applications are released to judges in the early fall (usually the day after Labor Day). A few days later, judges may begin contacting applicants, and approximately a week after that, they can start interviewing candidates. Although most judges adhere to this hiring plan, doing so is optional, so a few renegades do accept applications and hire their clerks prior to the prescribed dates. However, all judges using OSCAR must follow the hiring plan, and law schools are required to discourage applicants from submitting applications that would be received before the day after Labor Day of their third year of law school, and likewise will not send out transcripts or letters of reference before that day.

Competition is fierce on both sides of the equation: judges want the most qualified candidates, and candidates want the most prestigious clerkships. The hiring process therefore moves extremely quickly, and for the most part, hiring for federal clerkships is completed before the end of October.

Shortly after receiving applications, judges will contact the applicants in whom they are interested and schedule an interview for as early as possible. Most interviews are conducted in person, so you should be prepared to travel to meet with the judge, but occasionally, interviews are conducted via video conferencing or over the phone. The interview is a very heavily weighted portion of the hiring process. Most law firms employ hundreds of people, so the quality of interpersonal relationships is not necessarily a priority in the hiring process; however, judges' chambers are small, and because judges work so closely with their clerks, they want to like them! They also expect to be treated with the utmost respect, so be sure to be decorous and courteous throughout the interview. Each judge will run his or her interviews differently (one 9th Circuit judge is known to serve tea and cookies, whereas others are notoriously less friendly), but usually, you will meet with both the judge and his or her current law clerks. Judges tend to rely on their current clerks' opinions about applicants as much as they count on these individuals for legal advice, so approach any interviews you might have with clerks as seriously as you would your time with the judge.

Federal judges frequently extend a job offer to an applicant at the conclusion of the interview, and they often expect an on-the-spot decision. As a result, some judges may fill all their available positions in a single day, even if they have subsequent interviews scheduled. When booking interviews, judges should clarify the policies and procedures they follow, so applicants can make an informed decision as to whether to accept the interview. Once you have received a few offers, think hard about your decision and choose carefully—just as the judge wants to like you, you should make sure that the judge for whom you elect to clerk is the best fit for you.

OTHER JOB ALTERNATIVES

Discussing in depth all the many careers people with law degrees go on to have would be beyond the scope of this chapter, but there are some other common job paths law students follow for summer positions and beyond. One is clerking at a state or local level. These positions are less competitive than federal clerkships and are often available to students during summers. Grades and journal participation remain important qualifications for hiring, but the parameters are not as strict. For example, even if your grades do not place you at the very top of your class, your chances of obtaining a state clerkship position are still good. In addition, a greater number of state clerkships are available, and because the very top students tend to concentrate on landing federal positions instead, competition for state clerkships can be less intense—however, this varies from state to state (for example, New York state clerkships are always rather competitive). State judges require that candidates submit the same application materials as federal judges demand (i.e., cover letter, résumé, transcripts, and letters of reference), but the hiring process is decentralized and varies from state to state. Vermont Law School maintains a handbook with up-to-date information on each state's deadlines and requirements. Although these positions lack some of the prestige of their federal counterparts, the law students who fill these roles still gain valuable legal experience and have the opportunity to build connections within the judicial circle.

Another option is a position within the world of nonprofit public interest law. If corporate law is not a cause you are passionate about, you can take your legal talents to a wide variety of organizations, ranging from large national organizations, such as the American Civil Liberties Union (ACLU), to small, local groups, such as Pace University's Women's Justice Center. While summer positions at well-known nonprofits can be as competitive as big firm jobs and permanent positions can be nearly impossible to get straight out of law school, smaller public interest organizations are often thrilled to have the support during the summer months. The downside is that these jobs do not pay much, if at all. Some schools have funding to support students who choose to enter the nonprofit world; in fact, some even have student loan forgiveness programs for graduates who take permanent positions in the public interest sector. The bottom line is, you can do a lot with a law degree, so keep an open mind and explore your options.

CHAPTER 8

WHAT WILL MY LEGAL CAREER LOOK LIKE?

"I had no idea what being a lawyer meant until I spent my summer at a law firm."

"I don't think any of my colleagues knew what a transactional lawyer did until the end of 1L."

"I didn't know anything about corporate law until I was getting assignments from more senior associates."

These quotes—and we could actually go on because we have many more—are from practicing lawyers we interviewed for this book who either work now or have worked at a major corporate law firm. Many who aspire to be a partner at a top firm seemingly enter law school not really understanding what that life will be like, not even knowing what lawyers do on a day-to-day basis at all. Therefore, we are going to try to give you a window into what being a practicing lawyer in the early stages of one's career truly involves, in a variety of different environments, via first-person accounts. In this chapter, we profile lawyers in the following roles:

- First-year transactional lawyer in the project finance department at a major firm

- Junior associate with an international organization, working on a war crimes prosecution

- Fifth-year associate in the mergers and acquisitions department at a major law firm

- First-year litigation associate at a major firm

- In-house council at a nonprofit organization

- Of counsel at an international firm

- Partner at an international firm—intellectual property

§ LAW FIRM STRUCTURE AND ROLES

Let us begin by explaining the primary roles lawyers fill within a firm and the structure within which these individuals function at most major law firms, which is actually a very simple model: a pyramid. New associates join the firm each year and slowly they—if we may be somewhat blunt about it—get whittled away until the group becomes smaller and smaller. Some of these survivors ultimately make it to the top, at which point they become equity partners. Others might not make it quite to the top and become instead "service partners" or "of counsels." The base of the pyramid is replenished each year by individuals coming right out of law school, and so the cycle continues....

ASSOCIATE

To grossly oversimplify, partners delegate and associates work. Partners see the forest and associates see the trees. What those trees look like depends on the type of law being practiced, of course, but associates (sometimes called "junior associates" or just "juniors") generally fulfill research tasks. For example, a transactional associate staffed on a merger might be asked to comb through lists of clients and match them with invoices to ensure that payments are legitimate, while a litigation associate on a case might be tasked with sifting through millions of emails, looking for that "smoking gun." "The associate is the heart and soul of client service," a counsel at a major international law firm explained to jdMission. From day one, associates are basically hardworking apprentices, learning how to manage intense workloads and their partners' expectations to make their work more efficient and thus be assigned more tasks. With time, the lawyers who survive and thrive in these roles gain valuable experience and may even become senior associates.

SENIOR ASSOCIATE

At bigger firms, the pyramid is obviously larger, and associates report to a senior associate, who is in constant contact with, and answers directly to, one of the firm's partners. The senior associate manages the juniors (i.e., lower-level associates) and checks their work, such as going over a contract that a junior associate has conformed (a fancy word for "cut, pasted, and altered ever so slightly") to ensure that all names and dates have been properly changed. As the senior associate gains the partner's confidence, he or she becomes increasingly instrumental in managing tasks and may, if he or she is a transactional attorney, participate in drafting agreements or negotiating smaller aspects of a deal. If the senior associate is a litigator, he or she may negotiate with opposing counsel or argue minor points before the court. After approximately eight years—a very long, but nonetheless standard apprenticeship—senior associates (or associates in smaller firms without senior associates) can become partners if they make the cut.

PARTNER

To go back to the forest and the trees analogy, partners, as we noted, see the forest—the big picture. Partners are not a firm's "worker bees" (as one associate we interviewed referred to his brethren), but instead apply their depth of experience to broadly managing important client matters and advising associates and senior associates on the proper steps to take. Do not, however, take this to mean that partners at large firms are not required to work hard, just that their time is spent on higher-level responsibilities rather than mundane research and diligence tasks. In the end, partners bear the ultimate responsibility for the satisfaction of the firm's clients. Considering that the accounts in question at major law firms can often be quite large and that clients pay firms a substantial amount of money to manage them (and clients are becoming increasingly budget conscious), the pressure on partners is extraordinary, as is the need to get things right. But where there is pressure, there is risk, and where there is risk, there is reward—thus the huge paydays for partners at a major firms.

Beyond their client work, partners have to balance their internal managerial responsibilities with the important task of attracting new clients to the firm. Although this may seem obvious, law firms are not in business just to benevolently mete out justice. Like other *businesses*, they must constantly acquire new clients to sustain themselves. Clients whose issues or projects have been resolved or completed—not to mention those who have been lured away by other firms—must be replaced for a firm to maintain a constant revenue stream. Senior/experienced associates who display strong business development skills are therefore typically the ones who become partners. After all, the existing partners want to protect their profits, which is why juniors must pay such incredible dues—in the form of eight years of legal work and a track record or promise of business development—just for the right to buy (yes, *buy*, as in, *invest their own money*) into the firm.

COUNSEL

Many seasoned associates may have performed excellent work for a firm for years but still cannot make the leap to partner, because they simply do not have the knack for business development. Some of these lawyers may be aware that they work better behind a desk rather than with clients and will therefore choose to remain with their firm without being admitted into its partnership. In turn, the firms may wish to retain these extremely experienced, capable, and valuable lawyers into whom they have invested years of training. As a result, these individuals may fall into a middle ground between partners and associates and be assigned a "counsel" or "of counsel" role. In some ways, these individuals could be considered permanent senior associates—they are reliable, dependable, and paid well for their hours without being expected to fulfill the business development responsibilities required of partners.

However, a counsel jdMission interviewed described yet another way the position can work, saying, "I am a retired judge, and I want to do some mediation. It is your honor to have me on your letterhead, and I will use your office space and have some martinis at lunch and make you look good." Although this role is not available to lawyers coming right out of law school, it could be a fantastic lifestyle aspiration for much further down the road. An of counsel could also be an experienced lawyer who has been lured from another firm and is on the cusp of being offered a partnership position—he or she just needs to bring in a few more clients to prove that he or she deserves a share of the firm—and thus of its profits.

§ The Life of a Lawyer: In Their Own Words

We have tried to offer some generalities about what lawyers do, but we think stepping aside and letting the lawyers tell you themselves would be even more informative. For this chapter, we spoke primarily with junior lawyers, who graciously shared their experiences with us. However, we must stress that no one account can accurately convey what "all" lawyers go through. Juniors, even within the same firm, can have vastly different experiences, depending on who is giving them work and how, the amount of work generated by different departments, who the clients are, and other such factors. Still, the vignettes we present in this section should provide a bit of an overview to help you better grasp what you yourself may encounter once you have earned your JD and begin work for a firm. And, as you may have already guessed, certain information in these stories has been redacted, names have been changed, cases have been slightly obscured, and other alterations made to protect the confidentiality of our contributors.

First-Year Transactional Lawyer in the Project Finance Department at a Major Firm

"Try keeping seven checklists of 35 different things going simultaneously!"

Because junior lawyers are somewhat of a commodity, the environment among first-year attorneys at major firms is quite competitive. So, when junior lawyers finally start at their firms, many are fearful of stepping out of the lines, fearful of asking questions. Because of this, many do not define their careers. Most young law-

yers take what they are given and can get pigeonholed in a very narrow area. I think that many can "accidentally" develop expertise because they get staffed on a few deals and get good at one thing. Then, senior associates keep coming back to them for that one thing, and it keeps getting reinforced. They wake up six years in and realize they don't like doing regulatory work, for example, and can't make a change.

In my case, I very politely and diplomatically asked to be on project finance transactions, and that is what I am working on and I love it. If I got placed in the tax department, I would probably quit—I think that a lot of lawyers burn out because they are in the wrong areas and don't know it. They feel powerless and they might like some other part of the law.

With respect to project finance, let's say that, hypothetically, a client of our firm's is buying a power plant. We will conduct due diligence on the asset. We will have to put on our client's hat—like we are their in-house council—and ask all the questions that they want to ask and some that they might not even know they should ask. In this case, as a firm, we will have to make sure that the deal is sound from a variety of perspectives—will regulators agree? Will banks loan us the money? At times, we have to consider how shareholders will react. And we have to ensure that our clients are prepared for a deal to go through or not to go through.

From a project finance perspective, we might need to consider hundreds of contingencies in a credit agreement. Maybe my client is borrowing money from a bank to complete the purchase of an asset and I am staring at a 200-page credit agreement. I am definitely not going to be negotiating the terms of the agreement—that is for very senior associates and mostly for partners. However, I will have to read and understand the agreement, so I will be examining the agreement and looking at precedent agreements. I won't be writing new language, but I will need to be familiar with past agreements and "conform them" to this one. I will take exhibits, schedules, and guarantees from an old deal and adapt them for the new deal, and they will be reviewed by those senior to me and might make it into the final deal—at a minimum, it will make it easier to construct this one.

I will also make a checklist of all of the conditions in the agreement—maybe 35 of them—that need to be met before we can advise our client to sign the agreement. I will be tracking that agreement and making sure that we don't miss the little things. But I might be doing these things on anywhere between two and seven other agreements at a time, constantly assimilating all of the details from all of the various deals simultaneously. Try keeping seven checklists of 35 different things going simultaneously! And, of course, the details are different for each deal—in one we might be representing a company, in another an investor, and in another the bank itself. In one, a company may be buying an existing asset and in another, it may be paying a party to build and hand over a turnkey operation. Each deal requires that we analyze different perspectives, from who is purchasing the energy to liabilities if construction is delayed, etc.

I categorize my days in three ways: not busy, comfortably busy, ridiculously busy. When I am not busy, my day might start at 9:30 a.m. and last until 6:30 p.m. When I am comfortably busy, I am well staffed and working from 9:30 a.m. to 9:00 p.m. If a deal is pending, and it is urgent that we get it done, I am going to be starting at 9:30 a.m. and working until 12:00 a.m.—sometimes later—for one to three weeks at a time. Because I am not afraid to ask questions and ask for advice from those senior to me, I feel like I am pretty efficient.

JUNIOR ASSOCIATE WITH AN INTERNATIONAL ORGANIZATION WORKING ON A WAR CRIMES PROSECUTION

"It was two surreal years, and it almost feels like it was not my life."

We interviewed a junior associate at a major New York law firm who explained, as we noted earlier, that many associates do not truly understand what practicing law is about: "A lot of law students think they will walk out of law school and will be arguing cases in the Hague. Those jobs are one in a million." He is right—such opportunities are exceedingly rare—but we managed to find someone who was able to land such a job. Keep in mind, then, that even though this individual's experience is interesting, it is also highly unusual.

I graduated into a rough employment environment, and my start was delayed after graduation, which I saw as a major opportunity. I went traveling to [where my parents were from]. *Before I got there, I was in touch with Lawyers Without Borders, and my firm helped facilitate some contacts for me, too. I showed up in* [country] *and offered six months of free services. For an underresourced international organization, I guess it was pretty appealing to get a top graduate for free, and the next thing I knew, I was helping to make a genocide case against an alleged war criminal.*

My main task was to go through thousands and thousands of witness statements in a database, day in and day out, searching for mentions of the accused or any relevant information that may be connected to the accused. I had to organize the information and create a huge summary chart, detailing what was important and what was not. I wanted to assemble important information and also save others down the road time, by carefully cataloguing the information. Ultimately, I found 100 statements that identified this person in a way that was helpful to the case. Then, I went to [country] *and took new witness statements.*

In the end, we drafted a 24-count indictment and waited two months before the court ruled that there was enough evidence to proceed. I started to see that the six months was going to expand and was in frequent contact with my firm to ensure that I could stick with this work and not burn bridges back home. Soon, I was in pretrial, meeting witnesses and reading and responding to motions. At first, I was clueless. I literally had no idea how to respond. Eventually, I could respond, knowing that X is crazy and Y has no precedent. I was kind of amazed—Wow, what I am doing here is going to the international criminal court!

On my team, I became known as the "motion machine" and made and dealt with opposing motions. I actually took witnesses in front of the court. I am back home practicing, and we are awaiting the verdict. It was two surreal years, and it almost feels like it was not my life. I am not sure how it happened, but I got on the case very early and I offered to work for free—that had to be the key.

FIFTH-YEAR ASSOCIATE IN THE MERGERS AND ACQUISITIONS DEPARTMENT AT A MAJOR LAW FIRM

> *"A deal is like a fire hose. Everyone is just holding on."*

Law is very unpredictable. It is not like a normal office job. It can be very quiet for a few days and then a deal will near its close and you are on. If I could draw an analogy, a live deal is like a fire hose. Everyone is just holding on, trying to ensure it does not spray out of control. You can't fall asleep, and you can't worry about frayed tempers. You just have to get the job done.

There was once a 72-hour period when I had three hours of sleep. When a deal is closing, you need to get it done and done well before it leaks to the press and the market gets wind. So, you need to be available when the client is calling, when a specialist on your team is calling, when anyone is calling and that contract needs to get done. A fully staffed deal might have 25 corporate lawyers coordinating everyone else—we might need to make sure the tax specialist gets his work done, the employee benefits specialists might be making sure the founders are contractually obliged to stay on board, that the intellectual property is not walking out the door. Imagine the environmental considerations if you were buying a Dow Chemical or an energy company. Imagine the risks. We need to consider thousands of contracts and liabilities. The legal department in the company we represent might do five or six transactions like this in a career—we have more resources, and we might do five or six each year. So, they depend on us to ensure that everything works.

If I manage my work well—work harder and smarter—I am doing 80% "good" work and 20% crap, rather than 50%–50%. "Good" work is negotiating a deal, which is pretty much done by partners, but I might lead on very small points.

"Good" work is drafting an agreement—our deals often involve a lot of money, a lot of jobs. So, I have to be very careful. I might have to make a judgment call about whether or not to file something with the SEC [U.S. Securities and Exchange Commission], *which could make aspects of my client's business public—strategic thinking is good. Crap is due diligence—it is hard on the soul. Crap is cross-referencing pages of a contract, making sure that each number is repeated in the exact same way a hundred times.*

It is not as much about skill as it is about desire and stamina. Very few people have the drive to keep going at 2:00 or 3:00 a.m. Professionals who can get it right day after day in that environment get paid for it because they are at an elite level, like professional athletes. Ultimately, when you are trying to progress in your career, it comes down to who can make the fewest mistakes. Will you give up your life for a deal? There is a difference between those who will put 16 hours into something and someone who will put 21 hours in. Think about the people who are starting at top firms—all really smart, top graduates. Only 3% will make partner. It is the elite of the elite. But you don't just need to be technically perfect—getting every document right. If that is the case, you might be a great "service partner." Those who make the millions engender trust in their clients, so they win business. Your clients know you really well and know they are taken care of; they give you the business because there is a bond. You may have grown up together, gone to college together, or come up the ranks of your firms together. You know that you can each help each other.

Right now, I gain more and more responsibility. I am checking the work of those on my team. I am drafting agreements for clients. I am interacting with clients on a regular basis. But the next step is to negotiate more and to help my clients make judgment calls. Should they give on X point? Should they try to take on Y point? What is each point worth? Lawyers are an unhappy bunch—a lot of depression, alcoholism. I like what I do. I enjoy seeing my deals on the front page of the Wall Street Journal.

First-Year Litigation Associate at a Major Firm

"I actually wrote a small part of that brief, which is very unusual."

My day consists of research and writing—dealing with the source documents of a case. I get my assignments from partners, who just stop in and tell me they need help. They want to know the law, and I will research it; then they will turn that into advocacy.

Let's say we were defending someone in a sexual harassment case. From me, they would want to gather the elements under Title VII. What are the elements that our client will have to prove? Later, we would get more targeted. Hypothetically, let's say it was a same-sex case—I would need to find favorable examples. Maybe I would need to quickly research 30–40 cases. If I find 3–5 in my jurisdiction and then I am done, that is a good day. A bad day? I can't find one. I can't say, "I have nothing." So, maybe I ultimately need to go back to a senior associate or partner with points against our case that might have holes and discrepancies.

Recently, we submitted a motion to dismiss in a case. It was a 35-page motion—I found 40–50 precedents that were incorporated in that motion. I actually wrote a small part of that brief, which is very unusual. As a third year, you become more trusted and experienced and start to draft more significant portions of language, but it is always fairly collaborative with the partner.... You also deal with clients more directly. Right now, no one wants to hear from me. I actually take pro bono clients to develop my skills, because they will talk to me—they have no one else!

I would say that for me, 50% of my job is research. That for me is the fun side of things. It is like being in school. Forty-five percent is producing documents— answering interrogatives and taking depositions. Research can get quite intense. Imagine if you were looking into Merck's liability in its disclosures around Vioxx. You might need to go through ten thousand emails; you might need to go through

215

medical records; you might need to depose expert witnesses. Finally, 5% might be trial or settlement work. A huge percentage of civil cases settle, because the risks are too high. If you have a $10 million case and a 50% chance of winning, there is a lot at risk! This is the fun part, but it is a small part of my job.

In-House Council at a Nonprofit Organization

> "At a law firm, I probably would not state my legal opinion at a major client meeting for the first four years at least. At my organization, I am hands-on every day, leading all of our legal work."

I spent my time as a first-year corporate associate worrying about typos and deadlines. Those days were completely governed by the transactions that I was on. Often as a junior, the work resembled herding cats—finding signatures, pulling documents, mailing documents, binding documents, proofing documents, and now and then, drafting documents. If I was working with multiple clients, I was often flooded with document requests. Often I was the messenger/envoy between clients, and when dealing with busy and stressed people, I needed thick skin, because being rebuffed both at work and by clients can be a trying part of the job.

I had to understand the relevant aspects of the assets we were acquiring, and possibly more importantly, all of the liabilities. Let's say we were buying a small trading platform that was solid, even though the company was not. We needed to know that the IT [information technology] system worked; we needed to know who was servicing the system; we needed to know what was licensed and what was proprietary; we needed to know how long service contracts or patents would last; we needed to know whether these IT contracts had provisions that would trigger termination of the contract on the event of the completed transaction. I would read tons of contracts and then produce elaborate charts depicting the relevant details for each of them.

It can get so granular, and admittedly, some people love that. I preferred the big picture behind the details, but in any event, you are paid six figures out of school to get the details right—whether you like them or not. Highly paid junior attorneys can be doing basic tasks like binding documents after hours, because certain documents could be going straight to the hands of clients. Support staff helps, but as someone said, if you want to guarantee a good job, often you must do it yourself. I have heard nightmare stories about pushing relatively easy but client-sensitive materials and responsibilities to support staff.

I enjoyed my position for the most part but had to make a quick move out of the firm when the economy turned. With the help of a couple contacts, quick legwork, and not a small amount of luck, I made a transition into the nonprofit world. I arrived at my new organization, not really in the position of practicing lawyer, but they had so many needs—and no internal attorney—that I just started to fill that role naturally.

When I first started taking on all this legal work myself, this level of legal responsibility was potentially intimidating. This was an established corporation, not a fly-by-night shop. And here I was, a hair under two years out of law school and being literally the last say on legal. At a law firm at my level, I would have had at least three layers of authority and legal review above me on any deal. So you may be wondering… What worked? and What didn't? Well, these considerations weighed heavily on all the legal issues I advised or signed off on, and frankly, the name of the game for the first few months in this role was simple but important: prudence.

Nonprofits face a lot of reporting requirements—tax-exemption requirements and government and philanthropic grants lead to paperwork. If I were in-house at a specific corporate firm, say a Fortune 500, I might work in one area, such as employment issues or patents. But the nonprofit world tends to be somewhat understaffed, which makes many job functions quite amorphous and a bit more colorful and interesting. At the law firm, I probably would not state my legal opinion at a major client meeting for the first four years at least. At my organization, I am hands-on every day, leading all of our legal work. As any lawyer could relate, the first order of business at the new gig was ordering Westlaw—it was that bootstrapped.

We have contracts that need to be standardized and then adjusted, depending on circumstances and parties. We have leases that are renewed, negotiated, and re-drafted. We have insurance issues that need to be negotiated for our operations. We have had multiple legal issues that I researched in broad and varying areas of the law. Occasionally, I might be dealing with litigation and managing outside counsel, and it may take time and mental space to contemplate tactics—negotiation and settlement or fighting it out in court. I have to stay up-to-date on a host of legal issues that are constantly shifting.

In case it is not clear from this description, mastery of particularized areas of law can be difficult—if not impossible—to achieve within in-house roles. But on the other hand, it is never boring. In my final analysis, the law firm provided a solid core skill set for running this kind of role, which is essentially a good sense of drafts-manship and business strategy. This is why—notwithstanding the gamut of experi-ences and current reputations of law firms—I still say get a year of two of experience there if you can. Trial by fire is better than no trial at all. The level of attention to detail, the fear, the dread, and sometimes the triumph of doing better than your best (or at least, better than the other side's) will serve you well throughout your career. And while you will likely be less stressed in your post-firm role than in the "good old days" spent there, the emphasis on quality and client service that may be found, if you look, will carry you well into the future.

OF COUNSEL AT AN INTERNATIONAL FIRM

> *"I would love to go home and see my pregnant wife and son, but I am going for drinks with the head of a trade association."*

What I do is really unusual for a lawyer. I started at a firm that was tiny, and I had business development responsibilities right away. In fact, I was basically told that I had to bring in clients because that was the only way that they could afford my salary, and this is typical for a lot of small firms out there—most firms are not thousand-lawyer international firms with enormous clients.

I won a few big cases at my first firm and developed a bit of a profile, and I had some experience with client development. I joined my current firm as of counsel and bring in $1.5 million in new business each year. My guess is that I will need to get to $2–$3 million a year to become a partner. So, I travel constantly and meet with potential clients, with new client generation on my mind always. Tonight, I would love to go home and see my pregnant wife and son, but I am going for drinks with the head of a trade association. A lot of what I do is not paid—it is a leap of faith, hoping that we get clients in the end.

I brought in a client: an international pharmaceutical firm, making inroads in the United States. This client is now dealing with regulations that it has never encountered before. Suddenly, the client is informed that it has run afoul of the FDA [U.S. Food and Drug Administration]. Then, the justice department gets involved and starts filing civil and criminal charges. Then Congress gets involved... I am suddenly working with our team to deal with the regulators and head to Capitol Hill to defend our interests and lobby. We manufacture in the United States and are growing jobs in one state at a rapid rate. Now I am developing an advocacy campaign.

All the while, I am managing their budget and ensuring that we don't exceed their retainer. If we present them with a bill that is beyond their budget, they could either not pay or fire us. If we get close to our limits, I might step in and do a few hours of work for free, so that our $900 per hour partner stays off the file. There is no way that the senior associate will step in like that, because he needs to bill to survive. You can do that when you own the client.

PARTNER AT AN INTERNATIONAL FIRM— INTELLECTUAL PROPERTY

> *"The practice of law is no less a business than any other."*

Since I started as an associate, I have always said, "I love riding up the elevator in the morning without knowing what is going to happen that day." I start each day with a mental list of the things I want to achieve, and I never get too much of it, because things come up. I am always reacting to the exigencies of the day, which keeps things interesting and challenging.

At my stage of the game, practicing law for ten years, I spend most of my day interacting with associates, instructing them and monitoring progress. Because my practice is varied, with both an advisory and litigation component, I have a large group of associates that I manage each day, anywhere from two to ten, most often closer to the high end of that rather than the low end. Right now, I am working on a big law suit on a mass copyright infringement—I have four associates working with me. Meanwhile, I have two working on another litigation piece and a couple working on the transactional side.

I don't have a structure where every morning people are coming in and asking me what to do—the assignment and timelines vary and are dynamic. So I have a constant parade of people in my office. If I have something new, I spend a lot of time trying to give instruction and make sure they know what they are doing. I don't want associates in the field, wasting time.

It is not always clear what a client wants, but I try to give my associates the best picture of the big picture. When I started out, there were lawyers who would assign a discrete task without ever giving you a sense of what the big picture looked like. It made associates feel like a small cog in a big wheel with no idea what direction that wheel is turning—this is a big part of why people leave the law in the first few years. If all you are doing is due diligence, drafting officers' certificates or prepar-

ing affidavits of documents, and you don't know what you are doing to serve your clients, associate life can be a very empty existence. I want my associates to feel like they are part of the process with our client, not that I am the client.

What I love about my job is that it is a constant teaching process for me now, just as it was a constant learning process for me in the early days. Still, I don't want to give the impression that the learning is over. Not a day goes by where something does not come up that makes me feel like I don't know what I am doing. Any time a client calls me, I think, "Now what?" That sounds like a tough problem, and I understand why they need lawyer. The main difference between me today and me ten years ago is that today I have a deeper store of information and experience to draw on when I try to solve that problem.

One of the interesting things that I have noticed in the past few years is that I actually have more demands for me to be in the office! As a fifth- or sixth-year lawyer, I had a lot more flexibility to do my own thing. I would travel and had my laptop. I was really able to work on my own stuff at my own pace—I had earned the freedom and flexibility, because people knew I would get the work done. Now, I am feeling a greater imperative to be at the office, because people need me. They feel that sense of security with me there.

One of the reasons that I need to build a great team is because I still need to get out of the office and meet with customers and potential customers. The practice of law is no less a business than any other. It is the middle of April, and I just qualified for elite status. This year alone I have been to London, Cannes, Tel Aviv, Jerusalem, Los Angeles, and Washington—at least ten trips this year. I go to industry conferences and spend time at law firms in other cities, trying to find sources of cross-referral work for clients who are operating outside their countries. It is not all power lunches—I give talks on legal developments in my field. Still, there are lunches, dinners, and drinks. At a conference, my day may start at 7:00 a.m. and end with drinks at 3:00 a.m.

These days, a very small percentage of associates make partner. The attrition rate is very high, but this is more the associate's choice than ours. The hours are tough. Many don't want to work that hard. The mountain looks too high to climb. Some never even intended to be partner, which is a dynamic that has only shown itself in the last five or six years. It used to be that there really was not any question that everyone wanted to be partner.

Today, a shocking percentage of associates come in with lifestyle expectations that are not realistic. There is a reason why associates need to work 14 hours a day, 6–7 days a week, 50 weeks per year. It is because the economic model demands it and the clients demand it. Clients don't care that you want to see a baseball game. Clients don't care that your cousin is in town and you want to take them on a tour of your old law school campus. It is not a 9 to 5 job that you can leave and forget about it. I can't forget about it, because people have entrusted me with some pretty big problems that they can't solve on their own. People pay a lot of money for a team of dedicated professionals, who they believe has a team that can solve that problem.

§ Why Law Students Do Not Know What Lawyers Really Do

Now that we have shed some light on the kind of work some lawyers do, you may be wondering why we felt the need to offer these descriptions. Interestingly enough, many aspiring JDs (of all people) do not actually have a full or correct understanding of the roles lawyers are expected to fill. But how can that be? The primary reason is that, as we explained in the previous chapter, law school focuses on imparting legal theory rather than spelling out the inner workings of firms and the responsibilities of their employees.

In a series of articles about law school and the legal profession that he wrote for the *New York Times*, reporter David Segal criticized law schools for not adequately preparing students for legal practice, noting that very few law professors actually have any professional legal experience at all, with the average among instructors at top schools being roughly one year.[1] Teaching from a practical perspective is undoubtedly challenging when your background is solely in research. Segal states with a sense of humor that law journals facilitate inane articles that serve only the academics who write them. For example, a check of the *Yale Law Journal's* November 2011 issue reveals the following two lead articles:

- "Outcasting: Enforcement in Domestic and International Law"

- "Prods and Pleas: Limited Government in an Era of Unlimited Harm"

To grossly oversimplify, in the first article, the authors present an argument for nonphysical law enforcement called "outcasting," which is tantamount to the practice of shunning. The authors suggest that this practice may be more effective than most people perceive, especially in international law. In the second article, the authors argue that the constitutional division of authority in the United States may actually be interpreted not as "checks and balances" but as a motive for the system to "activate" to move itself forward, through bargaining and negotiation.

Although we are not qualified to question the *academic* value of these articles, one has to question the immediate utility of them to the practicing lawyer in transactional law, litigation, or public interest law. Again, revisit the statements from the lawyers earlier in this chapter (and we remind you that this sampling is hardly comprehensive); not much within their day-to-day lives at the office—which is where most JDs end up—is academic, and none of it deals with either of these topics at all.

---

1   David Segal, "What They Don't Teach Law Students—Lawyering," *New York Times*, November 19, 2011. www.nytimes.com/2011/11/20/business/after-law-school-associates-learn-to-be-lawyers.html?_r=1&ref=davidsegal.

And, according to Segal, firms are becoming increasingly frustrated with seeing law students graduate with an education that is primarily theoretical, as a result of their having mainly studied precedent cases that shaped the law centuries ago. In response to such criticisms, Harvard Law School overhauled its curriculum between 2006 and 2010. According to the school, the new curriculum "reflects legal practice in the 21st century, adding courses in legislation and regulation and international and comparative law to the traditional curriculum of civil procedure, contracts, criminal law, property, and torts."[2]

Some law schools are already following Harvard's lead in this respect, modernizing and adding practical elements to their curricula as well. Segal notes that recession-wary clients are now asking that junior lawyers not work on their files as a kind of on-the-job training, which is forcing some firms to spend months training their recent-graduate hires on the basics of transactional law, including the procedures necessary for a firm to merge.[3] Meanwhile, several lawyers we interviewed for this book noted that part of the reason public interest positions are so scarce is that these organizations do not have adequate resources available to train new JDs and therefore opt to hire experienced lawyers instead.

§ THE TIMES THEY ARE A-CHANGING

For years, a law degree was seen as a ticket to a reliable job, but this has largely changed. Law has become a truly international business, technology has changed the profession, and a prolonged recession has led to once unthinkable layoffs at countless firms—sometimes involving literally hundreds of associates at larger firms. In this employment environment, aspiring lawyers would be wise to keep their eyes on trends in the industry. We spoke to several lawyers and identified a few factors that may affect your career going forward—some will be easier to manage than others.

---

2 "J.D. Program," Harvard Law School website, accessed April 2012, www.law.harvard.edu/academics/degrees/jd/index.html.
3 Segal 2011.

OUTSOURCING

As corporate clients attempt to rein in spending across the board, they are demanding more work for less money from their law firms. In addition, some clients are facilitating cost reduction by hiring less expensive firms located outside the United States—typically in India—to complete what one associate described to jdMission as "commoditized associate tasks." These tasks, such as routine due diligence and transcription, can be performed in locations such as India at a fraction of the cost clients would be required to pay here—the outsourcing runaway train truly seems to be unstoppable. The *New York Times* noted that $1 billion will be spent on outsourced legal services internationally by 2014, and the *ABA Journal* claims to have already identified a New York law firm that is sending some of its work abroad.[4] Combating this outsourcing trend is difficult, especially for a lawyer who is learning on the job.

We spoke with a partner who responded to our query about the changing dynamic due to outsourcing by saying, "The question is not, 'Is there anything to do about it?', rather it is, 'What can I do day-to-day to improve the experience of my clients?'" This partner even entertained the idea of using outsourced providers to improve service for his clients, saying, "There is room for us to coexist," but adding that for now, every file he is on is unique and specialized and that doing particular work is the best antidote.

TECHNOLOGY, GENERATIONAL CHANGE, AND WORK ETHIC

Technology has made some tasks much easier for associates. Gone are the days of poring through dusty old books to find an arcane passage that validates a legal perspective—long live the database that processes searches instantaneously! However, this same technology is fueling the outsourcing trend we

---

4   Debra Cassens Weiss, "Are NY Law Firms Outsourcing Legal Work to India? One Admits It, One Denies It," *ABA Journal*, August 9, 2010, www.abajournal.com/news/article/are_ny_law_firms_outsourcing_legal_work_to_india_one_admits_it_one_denies_i/.

just discussed, and technology has also created an expectation that lawyers are reachable—and thus on call—*all the time*. Some lawyers recognize that technological change has put their social lives in peril and acknowledge that that is an occupational hazard at top corporate firms. Others prefer to bury their heads in the sand and ignore the call, essentially jeopardizing their careers. We spoke with a partner at an international law firm who declared "generational change" and "entitlement" the biggest problems facing his firm, adding, "I know this because I chair our internal professional task force, and it comes up constantly." A senior associate at a significant international law firm told jdMission that some junior lawyers mistakenly feel that because times are tough and they are therefore receiving fewer perks, the firm has less of a right to their time. This senior associate shared the story of a partner at the firm who felt extremely frustrated by this attitude and was actually postponing his retirement because he felt he could not trust his team to maintain the passion and focus that he had always displayed and provided for his client base.

According to those we interviewed, however, a simple antidote to technological change does in fact exist: enter your career understanding the demands, and try to adapt to the values and norms of your superiors rather than your peers. Law firms are meritocracies, and those who feel entitled will not last, while those who are diligent will thrive.

INTERNATIONAL BUSINESS DEVELOPMENT

The legal industry in the United States is a mature one, but other countries around the globe are growing steadily, and as they do, so, too, do the legal needs of their businesses—not to mention the outside organizations that want to do business in these expanding markets. If you have connections or skills that can help a firm build or strengthen a clientele abroad, or bring that clientele to the United States, this will make you very attractive to hiring law firms. If you are interested in making partner at your firm, you should work on building your professional network *now* (even before you begin law school) and pay special attention to the international contacts you make along the way. Focus on establishing profound relationships, based on trust, so that you can use your contact base later on.

JOINT DEGREES/SECOND CAREERS IN GROWTH INDUSTRIES

Individuals with joint degrees and those who have gone back to law school for a career change (to pursue a "second career") will benefit when their areas of expertise are in fields relevant to those doing the hiring at law firms. A counsel we questioned about trends in the legal profession told us, "Law follows modern trends. Clean energy, technology, and health care are growth markets, because America will have to wrestle with issues relating to these fields for many years to come." He continued, "A maternal health expert who gets a law degree could be a huge value-add in health policy or an excellent lobbyist." We are not suggesting that you suddenly shift direction and pursue a completely new profession before going to law school. However, we *are* suggesting that if you are fortunate enough to have some specialized knowledge and abilities, you should market these skills and experiences when you are in the midst of your job hunt.

What may be more immediately relevant advice for most applicants is that if you have a passion for a particular subject or industry, you should consider a dual degree program and determine whether this path might be the right choice for you. In Yale Law School's Class of 2012, 15% of all students are enrolled in dual degree programs. Most of these students are in the combined JD/MBA program, but students are also enrolled in JD joint degree programs in forestry and environmental studies, divinity, and medicine. At Harvard Law School, students can simultaneously earn a master's in public policy, master's in public administration in international development, master's in public health, or a master's in urban planning in addition to their JD. We could continue this list, but our point is that opportunities abound for you to specialize, and many law schools will allow you to create a custom joint degree program if the one you want does not already exist.

GOING PUBLIC

In recent years, the governments of Australia and the United Kingdom created a stir in the international legal communities by amending their laws and allowing their law firms to go public or accept outside financing. Opponents of these decisions worried that outside money would corrupt the legal profession—that frivolous lawsuits would materialize when well-financed "investors" backed law firms, who could then use their resources to show that they can outlast opponents, thus forcing lucrative settlements. Those in favor of the change felt that it represented a victory for the "little guy," who may have been trying to keep a noble battle going but could not sustain years of waiting for a final legal ruling without outside support.

We spoke with a partner at a very small U.S. law firm who complained of these fairness issues as he pursued a class action lawsuit. "Why is Exxon Mobile, for example, allowed to be a publically traded firm and have the deep pockets to defend a class action, but my small law firm can't raise funds and we may have to go broke fighting them until we get a judgment?" he asked. "Why can't we finance our cases on the open market?" For now, the governments of Australia and England appear to agree with this partner, and some in the legal community are watching these firms as test cases. (Australia's Slater & Gordon, the first law firm in the world to go public, IPO'd at $1.00 per share in May 2007 and was trading at $1.60 per share in winter 2012.)

Will the United States follow? That is tough to know, and more than likely, you probably have more to worry about in the short term. Still, if it does, this could lead to consolidation, because firms will have access to previously unavailable funding and investors will demand greater economies of scale. Law practices are notoriously Machiavellian, but they may become even more so should this change occur. If so, you will need to keep a careful eye on your client work and another on the boardroom at all times.

THE ADMISSIONS INDEX IN DEPTH

As we noted in Chapter 1, "What You Need to Know about Applying to Law School," law school applicants can actually gain a basic understanding of the relative strength of their GPA and LSAT score at their target school(s) by using the school's admissions index—an equation the admissions committee employs to evaluate candidates on a quantitative basis. Perhaps surprisingly, law schools make these equations publically available. Why? We believe that because the equations are all so different, computing your final score will actually tell you almost nothing about whether you will be a competitive candidate at the school in question. Therefore, the JD schools do not have any issues with sharing this information. To illustrate how these equations can still be informative and helpful, though, we list in Table A1 the equations for 15 top law schools[1] and use them to compute the scores that a hypothetical JD candidate with a 170 LSAT score and 3.50 GPA would earn.

Table A1. Comparison of Aggregate Scores for a Hypothetical JD Candidate at Top Law Schools

School	Candidate's LSAT score multiplied by	+	Candidate's GPA multiplied by	+	Constant	=	Aggregate score
American University	0.03	+	0.04	+	−3.18	=	3.65
Boston College Law School	0.51	+	7.56	+	−43.88	=	68.81
Boston University School of Law	1.00	+	10.00	+	0.00	=	205.00
University of California, Berkeley, School of Law	0.87	+	23.49	+	8.47	=	238.75
University of California, Los Angeles, School of Law	0.03	+	0.35	+	−3.74	=	3.26
Cardozo School of Law, Yeshiva University	0.03	+	0.28	+	−2.40	=	3.35
Columbia Law School	0.05	+	0.56	+	−5.51	=	4.09

---

1   LSAC

Cornell University Law School	0.03	+	0.29	+	−1.91	=	3.34
Duke University School of Law	0.02	+	0.33	+	−1.40	=	3.33
George Washington University Law School	0.03	+	0.34	+	−3.36	=	3.44
Howard University School of Law	0.39	+	3.54	+	12.33	=	90.17
Northwestern University Law School	0.06	+	0.86	+	−1.34	=	11.35
Notre Dame Law School	0.69	+	8.44	+	−60.55	=	86.13
University of Southern California Gould School of Law	0.03	+	0.39	+	−2.17	=	3.44
Stanford Law School	0.02	+	0.40	+	−1.17	=	3.29

As you can see from the table, the hypothetical candidate's final scores are not easily comparable—they hardly seem to relate to each other at all, in fact. The applicant's 170 LSAT score and 3.50 GPA remain consistent, but the final scores generated by the various equations represent a very broad range, from a low of 3.26 to a high of 238.75. The equation is the only variable, and although we know the numbers that form it, we know nothing about what the final scores tell the respective admissions committees.

However, the equations *can* shed some light on which metric the school views as more important, and by how much. Without going into the algebra too deeply, you can isolate the LSAT score and GPA variables and weigh their relative importance. For example, by dividing the LSAT score variable by the GPA variable, you can get a sense of the value of an LSAT point in GPA terms. See Table A2, which uses the same data presented in Table A1, and simply divides the first column by the second.

Table A2. Value of GPA in LSAT Terms

Law School	GPA variable	÷	LSAT variable	=	GPA points per LSAT point
Howard University School of Law	3.54	÷	0.39	=	9.2
Boston University School of Law	10.00	÷	1.00	=	10.0
Cardozo School of Law, Yeshiva University	0.28	÷	0.03	=	10.1
University of California, Los Angeles, School of Law	0.35	÷	0.03	=	10.3
George Washington University Law School	0.34	÷	0.03	=	10.3
American University	0.04	÷	0.03	=	10.5
Cornell University Law School	0.29	÷	0.03	=	11.4
Notre Dame Law School	8.44	÷	0.69	=	12.3
Columbia Law School	0.56	÷	0.05	=	12.4
Boston College Law School	7.56	÷	0.51	=	14.9
Northwestern University Law School	0.86	÷	0.06	=	15.0
University of Southern California Gould School of Law	0.39	÷	0.03	=	15.6
Duke University School of Law	0.33	÷	0.02	=	15.9
Stanford Law School	0.40	÷	0.02	=	22.3
University of California, Berkeley, School of Law	23.49	÷	0.87	=	27.0

Looking at this chart, you will see that the Howard University School of Law, for example, places relatively little emphasis on the GPA. On the other hand, the Berkeley School of Law places a great deal of emphasis on the GPA. Having a GPA that is one point higher than your current GPA is the same as increasing your LSAT score by approximately nine points at Howard Law, whereas that one-point GPA increase at Berkeley Law would be the same as increasing your LSAT score by a whopping 27 points! So, if you were planning to apply to several top law schools at which your GPA was higher than the average and your LSAT score was lower than the average, you could use the schools' equations to identify and target programs that are GPA friendly, like Berkeley Law. Just to be clear, though, we are not trying to say that schools with an apparent bias for the GPA do not value the LSAT; they still have very high standards, but simply place more emphasis on the GPA relative to other programs.

We could reasonably assume, then, that the exact opposite is true at other schools—that the schools that value the LSAT scores more value GPA less. In Table A3, the final column shows our hypothetical candidate's LSAT variable divided by the GPA variable and then multiplied by ten. What this number represents is the value of ten LSAT points in terms of GPA points. So, at Howard Law, a ten-point LSAT score jump would be the same in value as a GPA increase of 1.09 points. At Berkeley Law, however, that same ten-point LSAT score gain would be the same as a GPA increase of only 0.37 points.

Table A3. Value of Ten LSAT Points in GPA Terms

Law School	(LSAT variable	÷	GPA variable)	×	Constant	=	Value of ten LSAT points in GPA terms
University of California, Berkeley, School of Law	0.87	÷	23.49	×	10	=	0.37
Stanford Law School	0.02	÷	0.40	×	10	=	0.45
Duke University School of Law	0.02	÷	0.33	×	10	=	0.63
University of Southern California Gould School of Law	0.03	÷	0.39	×	10	=	0.64
Boston College Law School	0.51	÷	7.56	×	10	=	0.67
Northwestern University Law School	0.06	÷	0.86	×	10	=	0.67
Columbia Law School	0.05	÷	0.56	×	10	=	0.81
Notre Dame Law School	0.69	÷	8.44	×	10	=	0.82
Cornell University Law School	0.03	÷	0.29	×	10	=	0.88
American University	0.03	÷	0.35	×	10	=	0.95
University of California, Los Angeles, School of Law	0.03	÷	0.35	×	10	=	0.97
George Washington University Law School	0.03	÷	0.34	×	10	=	0.97
Cardozo School of Law, Yeshiva University	0.03	÷	0.28	×	10	=	0.99
Boston University School of Law	1.00	÷	10.00	×	10	=	1.00
Howard University School of Law	0.39	÷	3.54	×	10	=	1.09

In the end, do not be fooled by the numbers generated with these equations; they really do not indicate anything definitive about your competitiveness. You will need to consult each school's individual statistics to best understand where you fit in within its GPA and LSAT score ranges. However, after identifying a few JD programs you might want to attend, you can then use these equations to figure out which ones seem to favor your particular LSAT score and GPA combination—you just might find one (or more) that is favorable to you.

APPENDIX B

BRAINSTORMING

In Chapter 2, we thoroughly discussed *how* to write a personal statement, but if you are like most law school applicants, you are probably wondering *what* you should write. Fortunately, we can help you with that as well. Before you even touch your fingers to your keyboard, you should identify a standout idea with which to work, and the best way to do that is by brainstorming. In this appendix, we offer an exercise and a questionnaire that will help you generate your best ideas.

§ BRAINSTORMING BASICS

When you are brainstorming, "more is more" is definitely the rule. The more exploration you do and the more stories you uncover, the more likely you are to pinpoint your most effective options for your personal statement and diversity essay. You may have a knack for turning a phrase, but this is not a blog post—you are writing to represent your life in a few hundred words, so we advise against choosing a weak story and trying to make it entertaining through the use of language. And do not confuse "weak story" with "unsuccessful result"—some candidates' most powerful essays are about times when they actually did *not* reach their goals or struggled significantly with something before achieving their desired ends. Be exhaustive. Spend many hours brainstorming and consider all the facets of your life. This upfront investment will pay dividends.

§ MULTIPLE-ANGLE EXERCISE

If you are without a clue as to where to begin, start with this simple and methodical tool: the Multiple-Angle Exercise. We encourage candidates to start their brainstorming at a broad level by creating a detailed list of their various "identities," as shown in the sample list that follows. You may initially be reluctant to list all of your important personal, academic, and community identities, but at this stage, you are brainstorming, so exercise minimal self-censorship. If you have an idea that you feel has any potential, jot it down as an identity. To better illustrate this idea, the following is a list of identities for a hypothetical law school applicant:

Identities:

1. Political studies honors student

2. Community baseball coach to 9-year-olds

3. Writer of 31 articles for college paper

4. Summer intern at J.P. Morgan in Sales and Trading

5. Board member of high school alumni committee

6. Peer tutor in college tutoring center

7. Amateur chef

8. Devoted grandson to 90-year-old grandmother

9. Supportive older brother to college freshman sister

Your identity alone is not your story, but among your specific accomplishments within each identity is where you will find a story worth telling. The next step of the brainstorming process is to examine each identity listed from many angles and break it down, identifying all your major accomplishments related to that identity. Here is a look at one of our hypothetical candidate's identities and the accomplishments he might explore further:

Multiple Angles: Community baseball coach to 9-year-olds:

1. Crazy parents consistently called my home and emailed me—had to find a way to discipline people 20 years older than me.

2. One player's parents never showed up. I became his de facto big brother, making sure he came to the games. Even raised funds ($350) privately for him so that he could go on a team road trip to a baseball tournament.

3. Asked by my community center to sit on "Umpires–Coaches Board" to help improve relationship between these two parties. Helped start the Umpire at Practice Program, which allowed umpires to visit practices and discuss rules with the players.

This candidate would then complete this exercise for *each* of his identities. As he does so, he will likely find that under some of his identities, he might have just one or two accomplishments, whereas under others, he might have as many as five or six. It really depends on the individual's experience. In the end, by breaking each identity into its components, the candidate generates an inventory of dynamic ideas worth considering for his essays. Undoubtedly, "Crazy parents consistently called my home and emailed me—had to find a way to discipline people 20 years older than me" is much more interesting and lively—and would therefore make a more effective central topic for an essay— than the simple statement "Community baseball coach to 9-year-olds."

Returning to our "more is more" theme, let us stress that you should not shy away from the personal side of your identities. "Amateur chef" and "devoted grandson" absolutely have value in the context of your application essays. Do not close a door before it opens—you never know where your most powerful stories might lurk!

Your brainstorming process should not necessarily be exclusive to your own memory. Consider discussing your experiences with parents, supervisors, colleagues, friends, professors (where appropriate), and others in your circle to generate additional stories and even to discover how others view(ed) you and your accomplishments. Simply put, sometimes you will not understand where you have shone, and others may see a quality or skill in you that you were not aware you possessed. These added perspectives will help create a fuller, richer picture for you to work with going forward.

§ Brainstorming Questionnaire

Once you have completed the Multiple-Angle Exercise, you should be ready to move on to the brainstorming questionnaire, which will help you develop some of the ideas you generated and perhaps even identify a few more. Start by taking your outputs from the exercise and giving each accomplishment a beginning, a middle, and an end. By doing so, you will create a comprehensive history of your achievements and a large selection of stories from which you can choose as you develop your personal statement. Thereafter, answer the remaining questions (5–14) briefly. Although there is no "right" page length for your brainstorming document, most candidates tend to exhaust their ideas somewhere around 15 pages. We expect that you will be surprised by the final output and likely pleased with the number of interesting choices you will have for story topics for your essays.

EXAMPLE

Organization/Dates of Involvement: *North Shore Community Club, May–September 2011*

Description of Organization: *North Shore Community Club is a small neighborhood organization that runs athletic programs for kids*

Role: *Baseball Coach*

Hours per Month: *25 hours per month, four months per year*

1. Accomplishment 1: *Crazy parents consistently called my home and emailed me—found a way to discipline people 20 years older than me.*

   - Beginning: *Volunteered to coach kids and was enjoying the role, but never imagined managing crazy parents, too.*

- Middle: *As kids were learning on field and improving, parents were calling me and texting me, demanding that their kids get more time, get special attention. Two parents fought in front of kids.*

- End: *Developed parental code of conduct; insisted that all parents sign it and met with each parent to ensure that they understood ramifications. Kicked out two parents who were not observing rules. Behavior changed dramatically. Kids and I enjoyed experience more.*

1. List your major accomplishments/achievements (not responsibilities!) *in each of your professional positions.* To the best of your ability, briefly describe the beginning, middle, and end of what would constitute a story about these accomplishments.

2. List your major accomplishments/achievements (not responsibilities!) *in the academic sphere.* To the best of your ability, briefly describe the beginning, middle, and end of what would constitute a story about these accomplishments.

3. List your major accomplishments/achievements (not responsibilities!) *in the personal sphere as they relate to others.* (e.g., helping solve a family problem, teaching a child to read, mentoring a coworker who is having trouble, etc.).To the best of your ability, briefly describe the beginning, middle and end of what would constitute a story about these accomplishments.

4. List your major accomplishments/achievements (not responsibilities!) *in the personal sphere as they relate to yourself.* (e.g., completed a marathon, published a poem in literary journal, overcame a fear of heights, traveled to 17 different countries, etc.). To the best of your ability, briefly describe the beginning, middle, and end of what would constitute a story about these accomplishments.

5. List any professional/community recognition that has been bestowed upon you.

6. Describe any conflicts you have had in professional or organizational settings and how you handled them.

7. Discuss any professional or personal setbacks or failures that you have experienced (not addressed in Question 6). Have you ever missed any opportunities, not achieved a goal, or disappointed another person?

8. List your primary hobbies and interests, past and present.

9. List five words or phrases your friends or family would use to describe you. List five words or phrases you would use to describe yourself.

10. List all the countries to which you have traveled and your reason for doing so (e.g., business or pleasure).

11. List any language(s) your speak aside from your native tongue and your level of fluency in each.

12. Briefly, what are your short-term and long-term goals after law school?

13. List the reasons you feel you want or need to get a law degree. How do you believe a law school program will prepare you to reach your goals?

14. What do you want to learn in law school? What will be your area of focus?

APPENDIX C

ADDITIONAL SAMPLE FREE-FORM ESSAY

My mother called me at the office. Then she called my cell phone. Then she sent me an email with the subject heading "Call me!" Panicked, I abruptly hung up on my client and immediately dialed my mom's number. "Mom, what's wrong?" I blurted, my heart pounding. "Is everything ok?"

"Your father is coming in from the cabin, and he emptied out the freezer," she responded in a tone that implied she was struggling with a serious dilemma. "Can he drop off a leg of lamb and a couple of steaks to keep in your freezer?"

My mother was slowly dying of cancer at the time and had obviously not considered the panic that such persistent attempts to reach me would cause. She had somehow found a way to continue living life with a sense of calm and normalcy that the rest of us in the family—especially me—seemed to have lost soon after her initial diagnosis. As a result, packages of quickly thawing meat in the trunk of my parents' Buick constituted, for her, a matter of urgent concern, whereas the rest of us fretted over test results, side effects, and her plummeting weight.

I loved Calgary and had moved back there after school, never, of course, imagining that my mother would soon fall ill. I was a recent statistics grad, working as a director of research at a polling company, but as my mother's cancer progressed, I found myself wishing that I had chosen to study pathology or oncology instead. I knew rationally that I had no real interest in wanting to be a doctor and that at best I would only have been one year into medical school, completely unprepared to save the day, but like most people, I guess, I wanted to believe that there was a way I could help, and I was grasping at straws.

One day, when I was taking my mother for chemotherapy, I noticed a poster for the Walk for Life, a 20 kilometer walk to raise funds for increased cancer research and better treatment facilities for our community health system. My mind immediately began to race. I knew I could walk 20 ki-

lometers with no problem, but I wondered how much money I could raise. How many people could I get involved? Once I had made sure my mom was settled, I went in search of a sign-up point and filled out the paperwork on the spot. When the woman at the desk asked what my fundraising goal was, I blurted out, "$25,000." She paused and looked at me kindly before politely saying, "The next highest target right now is $5,000. You know $25,000 is a bit ambitious, don't you?" I felt my stomach drop just the tiniest bit but replied, "I will do what I can."

That very evening, I hit the phones, tactfully asking for donations and for others to join my team. I called every one of my parents' friends before moving on to our relatives and then my own friends. Next, I asked my teammates on my recreational basketball and hockey teams. When I had exhausted those avenues, I took my first audacious leap and started asking the members of our opposing teams for donations after each game. I asked the man who cut my hair, the guy who serviced my car, my dentist, and every pizza delivery person who rang our bell over the next few months. Even though I had never baked before, I somehow organized—and made four batches of sugar cookies for—a bake sale fundraiser at my office that raised $271. One afternoon, I found myself sitting beside my member of parliament at a restaurant, and before our meals were done, he had contributed $50. I called neighbors, former teachers, and friends of my brothers and sister. My colleagues joked that I was going to start using our firm's robo-dialer—that they would answer their phones one day and hear, "Hi, this is Steven. I am participating in the Walk for Life and need your support." I found that with each non-robo call I made, asking for donations became easier and easier, and I realized that this was because I truly, and quite vehemently, believed in what I was doing. "I am not asking for me," I would say. "You probably already know someone whose life has been touched by cancer, and if you don't, unfortunately, you eventually will."

During my four-month campaign, I must have clicked "refresh" on my fundraising page five million times, each time hoping for another contribution. On the day of the walk, I arrived at the starting line with a team of 14 in tow. I had personally raised $27,643, and together my team had raised a total of $49,596. I walked those 20 kilometers beaming, and along the way, other walkers who had heard my story found their way to me to shake my hand. I knew my mother was waiting at kilometer 19, summoning the strength to finish the walk alongside me, my father, and my brothers and sister, who had flown in to be part of the event as well. When we crossed the finish line, someone from a local TV crew stuck a camera in my face and asked me how it felt to be done. "We're not done," I replied. "We will be back each year until none of us need to come back ever again."

A few months ago, I completed my third Walk for Life, walking across the finish line with my dad, my siblings, and my mother's friends—and with my mother's memory strong in our hearts and minds. We had a team of 25 with us that day, and we raised more than $60,000. We have helped the regional health authority purchase new equipment and have helped improve the quality of cancer care in our province. Although I continue to hope that one day fundraisers like the Walk for Life will no longer be necessary, until then, I will keep going back.

Appendix D

Action-Oriented Verbs

List of Action-Oriented Verbs That Help Show Accomplishments, Rather Than Responsibilities

A

Accelerated

Accomplished

Achieved

Activated

Adapted

Addressed

Adjusted

Advanced

Advocated

Allocated

Answered

Applied

Appraised

Approved

Arbitrated

Arranged

Ascertained

Assembled

Assessed

Assigned

Attained

Augmented

Authorized

Awarded

B

Balanced

Boosted

Briefed

Budgeted

Built

C

Calculated

Captured

Cataloged

Centralized

Chaired

Charted

Clarified

Classified

Coached

Collaborated

Collected

Combined

Communicated

Compared

Compiled

Completed

Composed

Conceived

Conceptualized

Condensed

Conducted

Conferred

Conserved

Consolidated

Constructed

Contacted

Continued

Controlled

Converted

Convinced

Coordinated

Corresponded

Counseled

Created

Critiqued

Cultivated

Customized

D

Decided

Defined

Delegated

Delivered

Demonstrated

Designated

Designed

Detected

Determined

Developed

Devised

Diagnosed

Directed

Discovered

Displayed

Distributed

Diverted

Documented

Drafted

E

Earned

Edited

Educated	**F**	Honed	Issued
Eliminated	Fabricated	Hosted	**J**
Emphasized	Facilitated	**I**	Joined
Employed	Fashioned	Identified	Judged
Encouraged	Finalized	Illustrated	**L**
Enforced	Fixed	Imagined	Launched
Engineered	Focused	Implemented	Learned
Enhanced	Forecasted	Improved	Lectured
Enlarged	Formed	Improvised	Led
Enlisted	Formulated	Incorporated	Lifted
Ensured	Fostered	Increased	Listened
Entertained	Found	Influenced	Located
Established	Fulfilled	Informed	Logged
Estimated	Furnished	Initiated	**M**
Evaluated	**G**	Innovated	Maintained
Examined	Gained	Inspected	Managed
Executed	Gathered	Installed	Marketed
Expanded	Generated	Instituted	Maximized
Expedited	Governed	Integrated	Measured
Experimented	Grossed	Interacted	Mediated
Explained	Guided	Interpreted	Merged
Explored	**H**	Interviewed	Mobilized
Expressed	Handled	Introduced	Modified
Extended	Headed	Invented	Monitored
Extracted	Heightened	Investigated	Motivated
	Hired	Involved	

N

Navigated

Negotiated

Netted

O

Obtained

Opened

Operated

Ordered

Orchestrated

Organized

Originated

Outlined

Overcame

Overhauled

Oversaw

P

Performed

Persuaded

Piloted

Pinpointed

Pioneered

Placed

Planned

Played

Predicted

Prepared

Prescribed

Presented

Presided

Prevented

Prioritized

Processed

Produced

Programmed

Projected

Promoted

Proposed

Protected

Proved

Provided

Publicized

Purchased

Q

Qualified

Questioned

R

Raised

Ran

Reached

Realized

Reasoned

Received

Recommended

Reconciled

Recorded

Recruited

Reduced

Referred

Regulated

Rehabilitated

Related

Rendered

Reorganized

Repaired

Replaced

Reported

Represented

Researched

Reshaped

Resolved

Responded

Restored

Retrieved

Reviewed

Revised

Revitalized

Routed

S

Saved

Screened

Searched

Secured

Selected

Served

Shaped

Shared

Simplified

Simulated

Sketched

Sold

Solved

Sorted

Spearheaded

Specialized

Specified

Spoke

Sponsored

Staffed

Standardized

Started

Streamlined

Strengthened

Structured

Studied

Suggested

Summarized

Supervised

Supplied

Supported

Surpassed

Surveyed

Sustained

Synthesized

T

Targeted

Taught

Tested

Tracked

Traded

Trained

Transcribed

Transformed

Translated

Transmitted

Tutored

U

Uncovered

Undertook

Unified

United

Updated

Upgraded

Used

Utilized

V

Validated

Verbalized

Verified

Volunteered

W

Weighed

Won

Worked

Wrote

A Day in the Life: Reminiscence of a Harvard Law School Graduate

§ A DAY IN THE LIFE...

1L

8:00 a.m.: You get up early to review your notes from the previous night's reading.

9:45 a.m.: You grab coffee and a bagel and head to class, lugging your laptop and casebooks.

10:00 a.m.: "Contracts" class. You are in your assigned seat and ready to go.

10:46 a.m.: You get called on to recite the facts of the infamous "hairy hand" case.

11:07 a.m.: You survived and your professor has moved on to someone else. As you listen to the remainder of the class discussion, you settle back and take notes.

12:05 p.m.: You head to lunch with a few of your section mates and discuss some issues from class, as well as tomorrow night's "Bar Review" at a new lounge that just opened downtown.

2:00 p.m.: "Torts" class. You are fascinated by the concept of the "eggshell plaintiff," the principle that a perpetrator of a tort must take her victim as she finds him—for example, a person who negligently pushes someone with brittle bone disease is responsible for that person's extensive injuries, even if the tort perpetrator had no idea that the victim was particularly fragile. This professor tends to stick with one student for the duration of class, so you can relax and just concentrate on taking careful notes to be organized into outline form later in the day.

4:33 p.m.: Settled into your favorite chair in the library, you begin tomorrow's "Civ Pro" reading and carefully brief each case, then begin work on a draft of your first closed memo for "First Year Writing & Research."

9:00 p.m.: You grab some dinner from the cafeteria and head back to your dorm, where a bunch of other students are hanging out in the lounge watching television. You weigh the pros and cons of going to your room to review your notes from today's classes versus taking an extended study break.

10:00 p.m.: After some socializing, you decide to review your notes before going to bed. Better safe than sorry.

11:30 p.m.: Rest up to do it all over again tomorrow.

2L

7:30 a.m.: You roll out of bed, shower, and put on your new suit. You have your clinic today, representing domestic violence victims on an emergency basis, and you usually end up in front of a judge.

9:00 a.m.: You arrive at Family Court and head to the clinic office.

10:15 a.m.: A client comes in, and you quickly interview her to prepare the necessary paperwork for a temporary order of protection, then hustle upstairs to try to get her in front of a judge before lunch.

11:57 a.m.: You emerge victorious. Your client will be safe tonight.

1:47 p.m.: You hurry back to campus, finishing your "Corporations" reading on the subway. You are not on panel today, so you do not feel pressured to read as carefully as you might otherwise, but you still want to feel prepared.

3:00 p.m.: You make it to class on time and whip out your laptop, using the mid-class break to squeeze in some work on the law review article you are editing.

5:30 p.m.: Black Law Students Association meeting—you are thinking of running for president next year.

6:30 p.m.: Dinner with a few friends and some time to hit the gym and unwind.

8:30 p.m.: You get back to your apartment, check your voicemail and are excited to discover that you have a callback interview offer!

9:00 p.m.: You start your "Intellectual Property" reading for tomorrow, trying to stay focused on your reading, though your mind sometimes drifts to thoughts of that callback interview. You push through on the reading, because you want to be prepared to participate in the debate about the length of a copyright that will ensue tomorrow.

3L

10:00 a.m.: You dash off to your mandatory professional responsibility class. Just a few requirements stand between you and your Juris Doctor, and this is one of them.

12:30 p.m.: You meet up with some people from your 1L section to grab a bite to eat and catch up.

2:15 p.m.: You pass through the student center and catch sight of one of the many bar exam preparation companies promoting their services. Although you are already signed up for a summer bar course, an odd chill still goes down your spine when you see these people. The exam looms larger with every passing day.

2:45 p.m.: You head to the law school independent newspaper office, where you settle in to put the finishing touches on your editorial about the weaknesses of the two-party ballot. Being on the *International Law Journal* is great experience, but you know you will not have much opportunity for this sort of thing once you start your gig as a prosecutor.

5:00 p.m.: "Psychology and the Law" seminar. With just 15 people in the class, you can really get into the issues, and being able to tie your undergraduate major into your law studies is a nice perk.

8:00 p.m.: Today is Thursday and you do not have class tomorrow, so you meet some friends for a few beers. Life is easier and the end is near, but you think you might just miss it all after you graduate.